Pinocchio

A Family Entertainment

John Morley

Samuel French - London
New York - Sydney - Toronto - Hollywood

© 1982 by John Morley

Rights of Performance by Amateurs are controlled by Samuel French Ltd, 52 Fitzroy Street, London W1T 5JR, and they, or their authorized agents, issue licences to amateurs on payment of a fee. **It is an infringement of the Copyright to give any performance or public reading of the play before the fee has been paid and the licence issued.**

The Royalty Fee indicated below is subject to contract and subject to variation at the sole discretion of Samuel French Ltd.

> Basic fee for each and every
> performance by amateurs   Code L
> in the British Isles

The Professional Repertory Rights in this play are controlled by SAMUEL FRENCH LTD, 52 Fitzroy Street, London W1T 5JR.

The publication of this play does not imply that it is necessarily available for performance by amateurs or professionals, either in the British Isles or Overseas. Amateurs and professionals considering a production are strongly advised in their own interests to apply to the appropriate agents for written consent before starting rehearsals or booking a theatre or hall.

ISBN 978 0 573 11345 1

Please see page 86 for further copyright information

CHARACTERS

Pinocchio, the Puppet
Old Gepetto, the Puppet maker
The Blue Fairy
Mr Cricket
Mr Antonio, the village Policeman and carpenter
Lampwick, his son
Mr Fox
Mr Cat
The Mysterious Coachman
Mr Fire Eater, the Puppet showman
The Circus Ringmaster
The High Court Judge
Harlequin
Columbine } Puppets in the travelling Puppet show

Boys and Girls as Village Schoolchildren, Urchins and Circus Performers in Funland

Adult Chorus as Villagers and Magic People in Funland

Flexible Casting

This Family Entertainment has been performed by as few as nine principals (with doubling) and a small chorus of juveniles; but it has also been performed with fourteen principals, adult chorus and juvenile chorus.

The script can easily be edited down to suit a small cast if required. The parts of **Mr Fire Eater** and the **Circus Ringmaster** can be doubled to keep continuity of the "baddie" role.

The gender of the characters in many cases can be either male or female so this play is suitable for all-male, all-female or mixed casts.

ACT I

SCENE 1   The Village Square in the Village of Collodi
SCENE 2   The Travelling Puppet Show
SCENE 3   The Field of Miracles
SCENE 4   The Courtroom in the Village Police Station
SCENE 5   The Funland Coach

ACT II

SCENE 1   Funland and the Funland Circus
SCENE 2   The road back to Collodi Village
SCENE 3   In the Village again
SCENE 4   The Seashore near the Village
SCENE 5   Inside the Tremendous Whale
SCENE 6   The Seashore again
SCENE 7   Back home at Gepetto's Puppet Shop

The above scenes present no problems. The Permanent Set of the Italian Village is used throughout Act I, except for the frontcloth, or tabs, used for The Field of Miracles.

In Act II the Permanent Set is first hidden by a cloth or a big cut-out for Funland and the Funland Circus and later by one for Inside the Tremendous Whale. The frontcloth, or tabs, for The Field of Miracles is used three times in Act II.

Act II, Scene 4 is either The Seashore or In the Sea—see page 77 for this easy UV alternative scene.

For suggestions regarding the scenery please see the section at the end of the play, where notes on costumes will also be found. Only the Chorus needs a costume change.

1990 revisions to the text of **Pinocchio**

After seeing many amateur productions of the play, and listening to Societies' comments, the author decided to make a number of revisions to the text to make the play more workable, with much more pace, and to create a slightly shorter evening.

It is suggested that UV is used in Act II, Scene 4, if In the Sea is used instead of The Seashore. (See Scenery Notes on page 77.)
A new list of music suggestions has been included in this text and the play is shorter for the exclusion of three songs (Nos. 5, 6 and 11).

Musical Numbers

Suggested Songs—you may well have different ideas but these below have all been used in various productions.

ACT 1
Song 1: *Swinging on a Star* (Chappell Morris) or *Poppa Piccolina* (Chappell)
Village adults and children

Song 2: *No Strings* or *He's Got No Strings*
Gepetto and Villagers
The *Tarantella Tango* music (from "Carmen")
Villagers dance

Song 3: *I Love to Whistle* (Leeds)
Mr Cricket with audience and adult villagers

Song 4: *Nutcracker Suite* (Tchaikovsky) or *Puppet on a String* (EMI)
The two puppets dance

Song 7: *Money* from ("Cabaret")
Mr Fox and Mr Cat

Song 8: *The Judge's Song* (Parody from "Trial by Jury")
Judge and Villagers

Song 9: *There's a Coach Comin' In* segue *Where Am I Going?* from ("Paint Your Wagon")
Coachman and Village urchins

Song 10: Few bars of reprise from Song 1 or theme song
For curtain to Act 1

INTERVAL

Sometimes songs 8 and 9 are joined and become *Join the Circus* from ("Barnum")

ACT II

Song 12: *Having a Wonderful Time* or *This is Our Once a Year Day*
Coachman, Pinnochio, Lampwick and Funland People

Song 13: *Join the Circus* or *Come Follow the Band*

Song 14: *Chase Music* from ("William Tell Overture")
The Chase scene

Song 15: *My Bonny Lies Over the Ocean* or *In An Octopus' Garden*
for under the sea cut-outs

Song 16: *Three Little Fishes* (Campbell Connelly)
Gepetto and three glove puppets or three seaweed-style girls

Song 17: *Together*
The Fairy and Mr Cricket duet

Song 18: Reprise song 1
All

Song 19: Finale reprises and the theme song
All

The theme song suggested is *Wishing* or *When You Wish Upon a Star* or *Story of a Starry Night*

The following songs might be of help as they have all been used in various productions of *Pinocchio*, and used at various places in the script:

It's a Hap-Hap Happy Day

Zippity Doo Da

There's Such a Lot of Living to Do

Join the Circus

No Business Like Show Business

That's Entertainment

Brush Up Your Shakespeare

76 Trombones (performed with tambourines)

Give 'Em the Old Razzle Dazzle

Put on a Happy Face

The Best of Friends from ("La Cage aux Folles")

I'm a Brass Band from ("Sweet Charity")

A licence issued by Samuel French Ltd to perform this play does NOT include permission to use any copyright music in the performance. The notice printed below on behalf of the Performing Right Society should be carefully read.

The following statement concerning the use of music is printed here on behalf of the Performing Right Society Ltd, by whom it was supplied

The permission of the owner of the performing right in copyright music must be obtained before any public performance may be given, whether in conjunction with a play or sketch or otherwise, and this permission is just as necessary for amateur performances as for professional. The majority of copyright musical works (other than oratorios, musical plays and similar dramatico-musical works) are controlled in the British Commonwealth by the PERFORMING RIGHT SOCIETY LTD, 29-33 BERNERS STREET, LONDON W1P 4AA.

The Society's practice is to issue licences authorizing the use of its repertoire to the proprietors of premises at which music is publicly performed, or, alternatively, to the organizers of musical entertainments, but the Society does not require payment of fees by performers as such. Producers or promoters of plays, sketches, etc., at which music is to be performed, during or after the play or sketch, should ascertain whether the premises at which their performances are to be given are covered by a licence issued by the Society, and if they are not, should make application to the Society for particulars as to the fee payable.

DESCRIPTION OF CHARACTERS

Pinocchio is a cheeky, badly behaved, puppet with jerky movements and high pitched voice except for his one line of dialogue when he finally becomes a "real boy". He has some emotional moments, for he has a heart. Extrovert male or female. It is useful, though *not essential*, if Pinocchio can dance.

Old Gepetto is an eccentric and kindly puppet maker, scared of others, but he becomes brave when defending and rescuing Pinocchio. He has a comical love-hate relationship with Antonio. He is *not* plaintive.

Antonio is the noisy and blustering village policeman and carpenter. He cannot control his son Lampwick.

Lampwick is a rebellious and cheeky juvenile delinquent who thinks his father and his father's generation are soppy, and (like most of the characters) he leads Pinocchio astray. Played by an extrovert male or female.

The Blue Fairy is middle-aged though she can be younger. It is a mistake to cast this part for her singing capabilities—it is an *acting* part—and if she feels she is not a good singer then her songs can easily be "backed" by the Villagers singing offstage. She is a bit bossy, though warmhearted, like an efficient governess with much urgency. She mustn't be slow or dreamy.

Mr Cricket is extrovert and highly enthusiastic in the Victorian music hall style of "Champagne Charlie" so he has stylized entrances sporting his green walking stick. He is a comically intense insect and works with the Blue Fairy as a team though he isn't as efficient as she is. Played by a male or female, he is warmhearted and "vaudeville" style.

Mr Fox is a cunning, smooth, yet seedy villain. Played by a male or a female. Both Fox and Cat are obviously gangsters.

Mr Cat echoes Mr Fox's dialogue; is an idiot and is cat-like in speech and gestures and is more stupid than his crony. Male or female (though female is better—perhaps even "Miss Cat the glamour puss").

The Mysterious Coachman appears to be a hearty rustic but this joviality hides a cruel heart. He should speak mainly to the audience, not to those on stage

Mr Fire Eater, the Puppet Showman is a menacing overpowering Victorian actor-manager and scares Gepetto, as he is a wicked villain, a sort of "Italian Abanazar". In this script, he is also the Ringmaster at Funland, but the Circus Ringmaster can if required be a separate part.

The High Court Judge is almost directly from Gilbert and Sullivan.

The Circus Ringmaster is crisp Sergeant Major style. He can be made into a female part wearing period riding clothes and called "The Circus Owner". In this script he is played by Mr Fire Eater but it can easily be a separate part. Most of the parts in fact can be played by females.

It is important that those playing the various "wicked" parts should remember that they are indeed wicked. They are not just entertaining characters who arrive in the story—they must supply the conflict.

Italian accents. If Old Gepetto is played with an Italian accent then the other characters would also have to have accents. The best idea is a mild Italian accent for Gepetto—he needn't sustain it except for exclamations such as "Mama mia", and the rest of the cast speak without accents. If the cast do speak with accents—and I have seen productions using this idea—the audience can't hear what is being said.

ACT I

Scene 1

The Village Square in the Village of Collodi

The Theme Song is playing as the CURTAIN *rises, the Blue Fairy is moving around the dimly lit stage and as she waves her wand so the lights come up to sunlight at her command. She points her wand at the Village School and at once the school bell rings. She waves her wand upstage and the Schoolchildren (each carrying a large spelling book with ABC clearly seen on the cover) enter noisily, fighting with each other, putting tongues out at each other, some still getting dressed. She taps the Police Station door and Antonio, struggling into his policeman's hat and coat, enters from the Police Station*

The Fairy waves her wand and exits her job done

Schoolchildren (*shouting as they run in*) You hit me—I did not—tick you're on—are you still getting dressed?—I'm not awake yet—stop hitting me—booby! (*etc.*)
Antonio (*blustering; loudly, over the Schoolchildren's shouts*) Lampwick! Time for school! The bell's ringing! (*He does his policeman knees-bend movement and addresses the Audience*) I may be the Village Policeman but my son Lampwick is the laziest boy in the place!

Lampwick enters behind Antonio. He carries his spelling ABC book, and is yawning and stretching. Antonio does not see him

(*Shouting, at the end of his patience*) Lampwick! Where is the boy?
Lampwick (*behind Antonio*) Morning, Papa!
Antonio (*jumping*) Oh there you are. (*He attempts to hit Lampwick*)
Lampwick Help!

To avoid a cuffing, Lampwick dodges about and then drops down on to all fours behind Antonio. He then crawls forward between Antonio's legs. Antonio picks him up by the ear. The other children watch and laugh, and the school bell stops

(*During this*) I don't want to go to school! I hate school! School stinks!
Schoolchildren School stinks! Hooray! That's right! You tell him, Lampwick!

They continue this shouting while the Adult Villagers (representing the mothers, fathers and older sisters and brothers) enter fast and go to the various children scolding them

1st Villager Carlo, why aren't you in school?

2nd Villager Gina, why aren't you in the classroom?
3rd Villager Tessa, you should be working at school!

Lampwick conducts the Children as they sing loudly

Schoolchildren   "Why are we waiting.
                            Don't need educating" *etc.*
All Adult Villagers (*shouting*) Quiet!

The Adult Villagers now sing with the children

SONG 1

A Production Number for Villagers and Schoolchildren

1st Villager (*after the number, pointing to the schoolchildren*) I'm going to do some shopping so you must go to school!
Schoolchildren (*rebelliously*) All right!
2nd Villager (*to the children*) And I'm going to milk the cow and feed the pigs and you lot just must go to school!
Schoolchildren (*rebelliously*) All right!
3rd Villager Because we've all got work to do, haven't we?
All Villagers Yes!

>They wave to the children who wave back and the Adults exit one side, downstage, Antonio exiting with them. The Schoolchildren and Lampwick exit the other side

>As they go there is loud dramatic music and the evil Mr Fire Eater (big pointed eyebrows and perhaps a beard) enters flamboyantly—maybe through the Audience. He is overpowering, swirls his cloak about and carries a badly made puppet doll. Green spotlight on him, thunder and lightning effects

Mr Fire Eater (*to Audience; with his evil laugh*) Ha, ha, ha! Ladies and gentlemen, Friends, Romans and Countrymen, I must introduce myself! I used to be an actor but now I own a travelling puppet show and—well—(*he recites*)

>I'll tell you all about myself
>In a rhyming metre
>I'm ruthless and I'm horrible
>I'm Mister Fire Eater
>And I do things in cruel ways
>So my name suits me well
>If any puppet disobeys
>I give that puppet hell!

(*He laughs evilly*) Ha, ha, ha—yes, I'm Mr Fire Eater and I'm here in this stupid little village to collect another puppet for my show. But will the puppet Old Gepetto's making for me be enough? What I really need is some amazing *new* idea for a puppet show—but what? I must make money out of my show—even if I have to scare people half to death—so

Act I, Scene 1

I'm not only horrible to puppets, I'm horrible to humans as well—especially little boys and girls. And I'm *ambitious*. I am *determined* to be the best puppet showman in the world—oh yes I am!
Audience Oh no you're not!
Mr Fire Eater Oh yes I am!
Audience Oh no you're not!
Mr Fire Eater Oh no you're not—aha! Gotcha! So silence you miserable nonentities! Now to collect the puppet. (*He looks at the shop*) Curses! Old Gepetto's not in his shop! If that puppet isn't ready I shall explode with rage! Here's one of *my* puppets. (*He holds up a straggly tacky doll with strings attached*) What d'you think of it, eh?
Audience Rubbish. (*Etc.*)
Mr Fire Eater I agree with you. I need a new one—that's why I must see Gepetto. But where is the old idiot? I'll go and look for him but don't you take things easy 'cos I'll be back! Oh yes, you pathetic peasants, *I'll be back*!!

He waves the puppet threateningly at the audience and to dramatic chords, thunder and lightning, plus a swirl of his cloak, he exits

The Schoolchildren enter with their leader Lampwick, still carrying their ABC books

1st Schoolchild (*to Lampwick*) Shall we go to school now?
Lampwick No! (*Pointing to the puppet shop*) Let's wake up old Gepetto—come on!

They run up to the closed shop front

Schoolchildren (*chanting*) Gepetto, Gepetto, let's wake up Gepetto! Gepetto, Gepetto, let's wake up Gepetto!

They bang on the shutters and open them up or slide them off into the wings. We hear a few bars of quirky music

Old Gepetto is revealed asleep on either the counter top of the cluttered little shop, or on a ramshackle little mattress in front of it. He has a night cap on his head and a nightgown over his everyday clothes

Gepetto Eh? Oh! Ah! (*He stands up, yawns, stretches and scratches—percussion effects at this—and his nightcap falls on the ground*)

The Children laugh

Lampwick Morning, Gepetto! Still sleepy?
Gepetto Yes I am. I was up half the night making a puppet for Mr Fire Eater. (*To the Audience*) Well, hullo! Or as we Italians say *Buon Giórno* Have you met Mr Fire Eater yet?
Audience Yes!
Gepetto Horrible isn't he?
Audience Yes!
Gepetto (*anxiously*) I don't like him but he's my main customer and he's coming here today! Without the money he pays me I'd starve!

The school bell rings

Gepetto That's the school bell! (*Chanting quickly*) One, two, three, four, off you go to the schoolhouse door.

The Children do not move

Oh you must go to school! You *must*! (*Proudly*) School made me what I am today! (*He poses*)

Lampwick (*cheekily*) And what's that?

The Children laugh

Gepetto shoos them away and they exit into the Schoolhouse door or at the school area

Gepetto (*calling out as they go*) "Going to school is a golden rule"—that's my message to you!

He bends down to pick up his night cap

Lampwick (*taking out a catapult*) And here's my message to you!

He fires the catapult at Gepetto's seat, laughs and exits

Gepetto OW! (*Clutching his seat, he jumps bolt upright*) Cheeky devil! (*To the Audience*) You'll never believe it but *that's* the Policeman's son! (*Watching Lampwick exit he can't help smiling, then he sighs*) I wish *I* had a son. I've got lots of little puppets but they're not the same as a little boy. I'd make a good father, I know I would! Oh well—it'll never happen!

The Fairy enters, smiles knowingly and nods her head several times as Gepetto continues

And I must get the puppets ready for Mr Fire Eater! (*He starts to take off his night cap and gown*)

The Fairy points her wand to the sky, and (though not seeing her) Gepetto now gazes upwards to a corner of the stage area, and not out into the auditorium. He is astonished. There are a few bars of glissando music

Great heavens! There's the Morning Star! Why nobody's seen the Morning Star for fifty years! What is it they used to say? "Morning Star up in the blue, make my morning wish come true!" (*To the Audience*) Shall I make a morning wish?

Audience reaction

I can't hear you. I'm deaf in one leg. Shall I make a morning wish?

Audience reaction

All right then! (*He talks to the sky*) Morning Star, I'd like to have somebody to talk with, and fly kites with and go fishing with! I'd like to have a *son*, that's what I'd like! (*Shouting upwards*) You're a long way off, can you hear me? I WANT A SON! I'm going potty, talking to a star. (*He laughs*) Besides, wishes never come true, except in fairy tales!

While the Fairy speaks, he returns to the counter, puts away his nightgown, picks up a puppet and a paint brush and starts to paint the puppet's face

Fairy (*to the Audience*)
>I've watched him and he's good and kind
>So here is what I'll do
>I'll promise that his kindness
>Shall make his dream come true.
>Many troubles lie ahead
>But once the battle's won
>He'll find his gentle dream comes true,
>*For he will have a son!*

Gepetto continues to paint the puppet as:

>*The Fairy knocks with her wand on the Police Station door — percussion effects — then exits*

>*Antonio runs out from the Police Station area to centre stage in a great panic, now in red shirt sleeves and carpenter's apron, waving his arms*

Antonio Help!

>*He runs back inside again, tripping up and falling on the ground in his panic as he exits*

Gepetto (*to the Audience*) What's wrong with the old fool now?

>*Antonio enters again*

Antonio (*puffing*) Help! HELP! Gepetto are you there? (*He dithers to and fro*)
Gepetto (*to the Audience*) He's my best friend. We've known each other for forty years. (*Shouting at Antonio*) Good-morning, you mouldy old madman!
Antonio (*shouting back*) Good-morning rubbish!
Gepetto Numbskull!
Antonio Nut case!
Gepetto Stupid slice of cheesecake!
Antonio Red-faced baboon!
Gepetto Black pudden!
Antonio Nincompoop!
Gepetto You lump of stale vermicélli!
Antonio Grey haired old goat!
Gepetto Hysterical old twit!

At this Antonio remembers that he needs Gepetto's help and runs across to him and dithers

Antonio (*hysterically*) You're right! I *am* a hysterical old twit! And you'd be hysterical if you'd seen what I've seen! Gepetto, I've been a policeman and a carpenter for twenty years but I've never seen a log of wood like this one!

Gepetto What do you mean?
Antonio It ... TALKS!
Gepetto (*marching to Antonio's house*) A talking log? This I must see!

Gepetto exits into the Police Station

Antonio (*to the Audience*) Now I'm not a fool. Well I'm a policeman so I can't be. But nothing like this has ever happened to me before. (*Blustering, about to burst into tears*) It's a laughing log, a talking tree, there's only one thing to say and that is—(*shouting*) HELP!

Gepetto has lifted his end of the prop log offstage. Now Antonio quickly enters his Police Station and lifts his end of the log and they both start to cross the stage with the prop log

Antonio is puffing and blowing and when they reach the far side he lowers his end of the log and wipes his brow with his handkerchief

Voice (*loud, high pitched, through offstage mike*) Heavy isn't it?
Gepetto (*looking at Antonio*) Why did you ask if it's heavy?
Antonio I didn't.
Gepetto Well, somebody did.
Voice (*high pitched and cheeky*) It was me funny face!
Gepetto Don't you call me funny face.
Antonio I never opened my mouth.
Gepetto Yes you did and you spoke with a funny voice as well.
Voice It's me! It's me!
Gepetto (*staring at Antonio*) You never moved your lips!
Voice (*with a very loud, cocky laugh*) Ha, ha ha ha! (*With a very loud comedy, sepulchral chant*) I ... am ... the ... talking ... log!

The two men look at each other and now realize neither is speaking so they panic

Antonio (*together*) AAAAAAAH!
Gepetto (*terrified*) AH! It's more than a man can stand!
Antonio

At this he runs across the stage to his Police Station, opens the door, collects a notice saying "I AM NOT IN", hangs it on a nail on the door, closes the door and then exits quickly

Gepetto has watched this while still holding his end of the clumsy great log, which he now looks at helplessly

Gepetto (*to the Audience*) Did it really speak to me just now?
Audience Yes.
Gepetto Then maybe it is a magic log ...

He lowers it to the ground, unobtrusively ensuring that the one end is now slightly behind the wings. Offstage Pinocchio slides into the hollow log

(*Standing behind the log*) Seems all right ... and it's a nice bit of grain ... (*He runs his hand over the surface, carpenter style*)

Act I, Scene 1

Pinocchio (*unseen*) Stop it—you're tickling!
Gepetto (*jumping*) It's got Dutch Elm Disease! Ho, ho, you're a very cheeky log! So I'll make you into a very cheeky puppet!

He sings "la la" to himself and turns to the shop counter, collects the mallet and a chisel, turns back to the log and starts to chip at its surface

It's a chip off the old block. (*Frowning*) What a funny bit of wood! Unless it's my chisel ... (*He turns away and holds the chisel up to the light peering at it*)

There is a sudden flash in the footlights and a crash from percussion

The Fairy enters, unseen by Gepetto who is now centre stage

(*Hearing the crash*) What's that?

The Fairy waves her wand over the log. It is pulled off into the wings quickly—revealing Pinocchio lying on the floor

The Fairy exits

(*Seeing the puppet on the floor he speaks to the Audience*) Crickey! I never carved that! I didn't have time! (*To the Audience*) D'you think it's the thing that spoke to me? You sure? Oh look!

Ratchet percussion effects as the puppet sits upright, swivels his head to and fro, then jumps up and walks downstage awkwardly. He then jerks his head and sees Gepetto

Pinocchio Hallo, Clever Clogs!
Gepetto (*surprised*) Eh?
Pinocchio (*jerkily*) You're a funny old man!
Gepetto You're a funny young puppet!
Pinocchio I'm not as funny as you are!
Gepetto Don't be cheeky. I'm old enough to be your father. Do you know my name?

In reply, Pinocchio nods his head fast and many times and there is a ratchet sound from percussion

Pinocchio Yes I heard it, it's a *nice* name!
Gepetto (*pleased*) And what is it?
Pinocchio You red-faced baboon!
Gepetto That's what that old fool Antonio calls me! My name's Gepetto. Only don't call me Gepetto, call me Papa. Others call me Gepetto, but you're special.
Pinocchio (*jerking his head*) Am I?
Gepetto Yes. You see, you're my son. Why are you pulling funny faces?
Pinocchio I've got tummy ache! I'm going to make a rude noise! Here it comes! (*He burps and pats his chest and coat*)
Gepetto Oh, you've got wobbly buttons on your coat! You stand still and I'll soon pin them on.

Pinocchio stands stock still like a scarecrow, arms stretched out at his sides and remains like this. Gepetto takes the mallet and "nails" from the counter and hammers "nails" into the big buttons on Pinocchio's coat, holding a "nail" against the button with his left hand and hitting it (percussion sounds) with the mallet

Pin ... knock ... pin ... knock ... pin ... knock ... there. (*He puts the mallet away*) Now what shall we call you? D'you like Mercutio?
Pinocchio (*violently shaking his head and shouting rudely*) NO!
Gepetto Then ... Cassio?
Pinocchio (*rudely shouting*) NO!
Gepetto (*to the Audience*) I can't think of anything else—any ideas?

The Audience are thus encouraged to shout "Pinocchio"

Pinocchio! How clever of you to pick it up! (*To Pinocchio*) You're pulling those faces again!
Pinocchio Yes! I'm a bit stiff standing here!
Gepetto Oh of *course*—you need *oiling*!
Pinocchio Yes I do! (*He tries to move*) I've set like a jelly! My hands look like fish fingers! (*He holds them up, fingers spread wide open*)
Gepetto Now where's the oil can? (*He collects it from the counter top*) Right Pinocchio, we'll start with your neck and than all your joints.

Gepetto "squirts" oil at Pinocchio's puppet joints and after each application, Pinocchio moves and eases his neck, his elbows, knees, wrists, ankles (percussion effects)

Pinocchio (*ad libbing*) Oooo—that's better—thanks Papa—oh that's easier—a bit more her Papa—oooo (*he laughs*)—that tickles! (*He eases himself*)
Gepetto Now follow me as I walk.

Gepetto walks slowly. Pinocchio tries to follow but he is gawky and clumsy

(*Alarmed*) Here! Don't waggle your head too much or your ears'll fall off.

Pinocchio wiggles about and tries to walk

Now try and jump.
Pinocchio What's "jump"?
Gepetto Like this (*He jumps, then gasps, holding his side*) I'm too old to jump.
Pinocchio But I *want* to jump! I *want* to jump! I *want* to jump!

He jumps about all over the place watched by the laughing Gepetto

Gepetto (*realizing*) Here—am I going mad? You're a puppet, aren't you?
Pinocchio (*with much head nodding*) Yes!
Gepetto BUT WHERE ARE YOUR STRINGS?
Pinocchio Haven't got any!
Gepetto What—no strings?

The music for Song 2 starts

Act I, Scene 1

Turn round! (*Examining him*) No strings at the back and no strings on top! (*Amazed but pleased, he sings Song 2*)

SONG 2

As the amazed Gepetto starts to sing to the jerky and staccato music, so Pinocchio dances or struts about jerkily

All the Villagers enter at once, point at Pinocchio, register amazement and sing

Gepetto does a couple of polka steps on his own, the melody is played loudly and to a definite "um-pom-pom" tempo. Gepetto sings "um-pom-pom" and shows Pinocchio some simple steps. Pinocchio laughs and enjoys this, so do the villagers. Now Pinocchio and Gepetto dance a comedy tango

(*Calling to them*) Anyone would think you haven't seen a puppet dancing before!
Villagers (*gazing*) We haven't!
Gepetto Well don't just stand there, do something! Help me to show him a tango because (*putting his hand to his back*) I'm too old for this sort of caper! (*To two Villagers*) Macaroni—Tagliatelli—show him a tango—go on!

The Villagers show Pinocchio various snatches of dance, to a tango tempo of the song

1st Girl Well we can show you a bit of a tango Mr Pistachio.
Pinocchio (*loudly*) Pinocchio.
1st Girl Mr Pinocchio. Come on, Dino!

Dino and Gina dance a few steps

Gepetto Brilliantissimo!
2nd Villager Mr Pinocchio, here's a waltz! Come on, Cassata!

Marco and Carla dance a few steps for him

3rd Villager Let's show him something noisy!
All (*loudly agreeing*) Yes! Watch this, Pinocchio!
Pinocchio (*very pleased at the thought*) Something noisy! *Good!*

PRODUCTION NUMBER

All dance to the same music now in a rock tempo or move on to a separate rock number. The extrovert Pinocchio "goes mad" as he dances about. Even Gepetto and the more mature Villagers attempt hand jive movements

The number ends, and the Villagers exit, all waving and shouting ad lib good lucks and goodbyes to Gepetto and Pinocchio who wave back

Pinocchio (*calling to them*) Thank you! That was good! In fact it was fabuloosa!
Gepetto "It was *fabuloosa*?" You're as bad as the other village boys! (*Proudly*) Yes, you're just like a boy! *My* boy!

But Pinocchio is not interested in this sentimentality. He has noticed the Audience and points to them, and grins

Pinocchio (*to the Audience*) I want to dance with you lot now!

He runs down at the side of the stage into the Auditorium. The House lights go on

Gepetto Hey! Stop! The boy's gone barmy! Come back!
Pinocchio Shall we tango, lady?

He pulls someone from a front row seat and attempts to make her dance

Gepetto Come back! (*To the person*) I'm so sorry, madam! Come back here you naughty puppet! If you don't come back at once, I'll smack bot-bot!

Pinocchio stops larking about

Pinocchio (*alarmed*) Smack bot-bot? Help! (*He runs back up on to the stage*)

The House lights go off

Gepetto Pinocchio, you'll be the death of me! You will! Come here!

Gepetto chases Pinocchio round the stage but Pinocchio runs behind the shop counter. He picks up a big knife and lashes out at some of the puppets hanging up by their strings and they fall off their pegs to the floor. He seems to be doing serious damage as he wields the knife and sings loudly and excitedly some of the last song unaccompanied. (Percussion crashes also)

(*Shouting furiously*) Pinocchio!

Pinocchio stops panting for breath. Silence. The fun has ended and he has lost control of himself and it is a grim moment

(*Horrified and really frightened*) What are you doing? We'll *starve*! These puppets are for Mr Fire Eater and he's coming to collect them TODAY!
Pinocchio (*not caring*) So?
Gepetto So, unless I sell these puppets to him I'll have no money! Money pays for food! Money pays the rent! You stupid boy! You ... you ... *Woodentop!*
Pinocchio (*quietly*) Please don't call me Woodentop. I don't want to be made of wood. *I want to be a real boy.*
Gepetto I'm sorry. I want you to be a real boy as well—(*angrily*)—but not a wicked boy. You mustn't do wrong.
Pinocchio Wrong? What is "wrong"?
Gepetto You don't know right from wrong? Then you need to go to school.

At this, Pinocchio groans and suddenly flops down, arms swinging about

Mamma mia! He's gone all dangly! (*Straightening him upright again*) Are you all right?
Pinocchio (*brightly*) Oh yes Papa!

But he flops down again

Gepetto (*helping him up again*) You need to take things slowly at first. Go for a slow walk in a straight line. (*He moves Pinocchio round so that he*

Act I, Scene 1

faces the wings) Now you're in a straight line, go to the school, SLOWLY, and when you get there, just turn round and come back slowly.

Pinocchio Yes Papa. (*Very slow deep speaking voice, in time to the slow motion robot movements*) I'll . . . go . . . for . . . a . . . slow . . . walk . . . to . . . the . . . school . . .

In slow motion with stiff movements, he walks offstage like a robot

Gepetto See you later!

Pinocchio (*deep slow voice*) See . . . you . . . later . . . Pa . . . pa . . .

He exits

Gepetto (*looking upwards*) He's naughty, he's cheeky, and he tells whopping lies but I *still* say "thank you", Morning Star! P'raps he *will* become a real boy and not just a puppet!

A drum beat shatters this emotional outburst

(*Scared*) That drum! It's Mr Fire Eater! And Pinocchio's wrecked the puppets!

He runs behind the counter and holds up a very bedraggled-looking puppet

There is a grand fanfare as Mr Fire Eater enters flamboyantly. He is overpowering and swirls his cloak, there is thunder and lightning and dramatic chords

Mr Fire Eater (*ignoring Gepetto and speaking loudly and addressing the whole world, laughing evilly*) Ha, ha, ha! Ladies and gentleman, from the depths of my heart I thank you most sincerely for your wonderful welcome and I . . . (*Realizing*) There's nobody here.

Gepetto Only me, Mr Fire Eater.

Mr Fire Eater (*with overdone charm*) Mr Gepetto! I'm delighted to meet you again and to say to you in a most cordial manner (*snarling and thundering*) WHERE ARE MY PUPPETS?

Gepetto They're not quite ready, Mr Fire Eater. You see——

Mr Fire Eater But you promised them weeks ago! You know I need them for tonight! This village is the start of my grand tour of Italy!

Gepetto Oh dear . . . (*Desperately*) They'll be ready by tonight, certainly, someway, somehow.

Mr Fire Eater Well if they're *not* ready by tonight, there'll be no more work! And if you don't work for me, who will you work for?

Gepetto No one, Mr Fire Eater.

Mr Fire Eater Exactly. If they're not ready by tonight—there'll be big trouble. (*Laughing*) Ha, ha, ha!

Gepetto pathetically holds out the bedraggled looking puppet. The laughter stops and Mr Fire Eater glares at the miserable thing

Is that for me to use *tonight*? Have you taken leave of your senses? Do you realize I've come ahead of my travelling puppet show specially so that I can check the new puppets I ordered from you? I'll take this one and I'll take it *now*.

He snatches up an attractive puppet

Gepetto Oh not that one, Mr Fire Eater. That's my best puppet. It's not for sale.
Mr Fire Eater It is now! Ha, ha, ha!
Gepetto It'll cost you a lot of money, that one will.
Mr Fire Eater It will cost me nothing. (*Threateningly*) And the rest of the puppets *must be ready by tonight. When I return they must be ready!*

He starts to exit but turns back and addresses the Audience

I'm not called Mr Fire Eater for nothing! I'm fiery all right! Oh yes I am!
Audience Oh, no you're not!
Mr Fire Eater Oh shurrup!

He exits theatrically, waving triumphantly the big and attractive puppet

Gepetto is left to somehow sort out the broken strings and his bedraggled puppet

Fairy music is heard as the Blue Fairy enters at once, unseen by Gepetto, and addresses the Audience

Fairy I know what you're thinking
And of course you're right
Mr Fire Eater
Has cruel strength and might.
Yet although many dangers
Lie in wait around the bend
Gepetto is so good and kind
He'll win through in the end!

The Fairy exits and Pinocchio returns walking in slow motion as he enters

Gepetto (*seeing him*) Ah!
Pinocchio (*in a slow deep voice*) I went to ... the ... school ... Pa ... pa ...
Gepetto Did you flop down any more?
Pinocchio (*in a slow deep voice*) No ... Papa ... I'm ... all right ... now ...
Gepetto Then you can talk quickly now, can't you?
Pinocchio (*very fast indeed, with odd comical jerky movements*) Like this you mean? Oh it's nice to be my own happy self again after that slow walk to the school and back and it's a nice day for a walkabout isn't it Papa and I feel every so much bet——
Gepetto All right! All right! You needn't go mad! Return to normal now!
Pinocchio (*normal voice and actions*) Yes Papa. (*Greatly curious*) What is a school *for*, Papa?
Gepetto (*piously*) School is where we are taught to be brave, thoughtful and unselfish.
Pinocchio School! Good idea! (*Turning away, as an aside to the Audience*) School, eeeeuuuuuurrrch!
Gepetto You learn things at school, like arithmetic. If I have four apples in my hand, then I put another four apples in my hand, what have I got?

Act I, Scene 1 13

Pinocchio A very big hand.
Gepetto (*disgusted*) Doh! And everyone at school says (*quickly chanting*) "One, two, three, four, off I got to the schoolhouse door."
Pinocchio (*with the same inflection*) "One, two, three, four, off I go to the schoolhouse door." If it will make me like other boys, I'd *like* to go to school Papa.
Gepetto Yes, you must be like all the other boys and learn to spell.

Pinocchio sniffs deeply

I said "spell", not 'smell'.
Pinocchio But I can't learn to spell! And I can't go to school either!
Gepetto Why can't you?
Pinocchio 'Cos I haven't got a spelling book!
Gepetto Spelling books cost money. Money that I haven't got. (*He takes his change from his pocket*) Two lire, that's all I've got in the world.
Pinocchio You've got me!
Gepetto (*drily*) Yes. Two lire. (*To himself, an idea occurring*) Ah! (*He collects a brightly coloured but patched coat from a hook on the shop wall and brushes it carefully with his hand and puts it on*) I'll get the book at the village store and ask them to lend me some money ... Oh well, I wanted a little boy and I've *got* a little boy so what am I worrying about? I'm not worried! Of course I'm not worried! I'm happy! (*He starts to exit but turns back at the wings*) I think!

Gepetto exits

Pinocchio picks up the mallet and chisel in the shop

Pinocchio What can I carve? What can I *improve*?

He looks round and starts to bang noisily at some puppets hanging up

The Fairy enters

Pinocchio (*singing*) La, la la. (*He sees the Fairy and is cheeky*) Who are you?
Fairy I'm the Blue Fairy. Pinocchio, greeting!
 You must learn to do good
 So I'm glad we're meeting.
Pinocchio (*pulling a hideous face at her and shouting*) SHANT!
Fairy You're a selfish puppet, you couldn't care less. Do you really want to be selfish?
Pinocchio (*proudly*) YES!
Fairy "Be kind to others" is a golden rule.
 Gepetto is buying you a book for school.
 When he comes back he'll have *nothing*, so—
 You will be kind and say thank you?
Pinocchio NO!

The Fairy is becoming tight-lipped and irritated by Pinocchio and she shows it as she ploughs on

Fairy You're a well-made puppet, good and strong
But I see you can't tell right from wrong!
You need a conscience—
Pinocchio A conscience, what's that?
Fairy It tells you what's right—
Pinocchio Don't want one; that's flat!

The Fairy is frustrated and tetchy now

Fairy Oh dear. Your puppet head is so thick it
Needs someone else—my friend Mr Cricket!
(*Becoming angry*)
So here comes your CONSCIENCE, you
obstinate dunce.
Yes, Mr Cricket, come hither—at once!

A few bars of typical vaudeville music and Mr Cricket suddenly jumps onstage. He is finicky in his movements and his walking stick is flicked about with style

Mr Cricket (*exploding with* bonhomie) Hullo folks! I'm Mr Cricket!

Taking his hat off with a flourish, he poses and remains stock still as he loudly announces

When you get in trouble
And you don't think you can lick it
Just call on me
Because you see
My name is Mr Cricket!!!!
Fairy Ah, Mr Cricket, a boon I crave
Teach this naughty boy how to behave!

Mr Cricket puts his hat on again

Mr Cricket Certainly madam! (*He salutes cheerily in a music hall style, and clearly emphasizes his catch phrase*) Certainly, certainly—certainly with a capital S!
Fairy I must leave you, I'm late for another appointment. And as we fairies say, I must fly!

The Blue Fairy exits on tiptoe, her arms waving as though in flight

There is music hall vamp music as Mr Cricket takes Pinocchio's arm and parades him to and fro across the stage

Mr Cricket (*expansively*) My boy, I am Mr Cricket and my boss is the Blue Fairy! Yes she's the good old B.F.!
Pinocchio Then are you going to——?
Mr Cricket (*ploughing on*) I work for her because what I represent is everybody's Conscience—(*emphasizing his catch phrase*)—Conscience with a capital K!
Pinocchio So will you be——?

Act I, Scene 1

Mr Cricket (*ploughing on*) Let me elucidate! I live in the green and grassy fields outside this village and I've been called here by the Blue Fairy to bring you a message of hope! H–O–A–P—hope!
Pinocchio Mr Cricket, I don't think that spelling is correct.
Mr Cricket (*indignantly*) Not correct? S–o–a–p—Soap. H–o–a–p—Hope!
Pinocchio I'm sorry. You're right.
Mr Cricket As I was saying, I've been called here to bring you a message. (*He stops and examines Pinocchio*) Son, here is that message. You want to be a real boy, but *you are only made of wood*!

He taps Pinocchio's head with his green stick—percussion wooden blocks effect—then he parades with Pinocchio again

We've got a lot of work to do together so listen. L–I–Double S–E–N ... Lissen.

There is a burst of fairy music and Mr Cricket moralizes over it, making a sweeping gesture with his hand

Be brave and truthful and unselfish, then one day you'll stop being a puppet and become a real live boy.
Pinocchio (*thrilled*) A real live boy?
Mr Cricket Definitely! Mind you at the moment you can't even tell the difference between right and wrong!
Pinocchio Wrong with a capital R?
Mr Cricket (*tremendously pleased at this*) My boy, I'm so proud of you and you're spelling! You're learning fast! Do what I do, say what I say, and you'll go far!

There are percussion beats under his chant

> If I'm ever worried
> If I'm ever blue
> Here's the little something
> That I like to do!

The Lights go down to a spotlight on Mr Cricket and he sings as though he is Champagne Charlie in a music hall

SONG 3

After his chorus the vaudeville music continues quietly and he speaks over it

Now, Pinocchio, first thing is to *learn* how to whistle. Pucker your lips— that's it—breathe in—that's it—now blow!

Pinocchio blows, but nothing happens

Once again!

Still no sound from Pinocchio

There's a well-known phrase we cricketing folk use. "Wet your whistle"! Try wetting yours! (*He watches Pinocchio trying to whistle*) My boy, that's wetter and wetter and better and better. So!

He gestures towards Pinocchio like a conjuror's assistant and Pinocchio manages a feeble whistle

I'm afraid not, my boy. You need some phlegm—phlegm—with a capital F. (*Uncertainly*) I'm not too good at whistling myself ... I wonder who could show you ... (*He notices the Audience*) Will you? Don't shout all at once! Come on, everybody—undo your belts and belt it out! One ... two ... three ... Whistle!

The Audience whistles

Good! Good! And it's bound to get better! Show Pinocchio again—very loud this time! (*He conducts them*) One ... two ... three...!

The Audience gives another whistle

That was windy and wonderful! I like enthusiasm—enthusiasm with a capital I! (*To Pinocchio*) Those good people out there have inspired you, so try again!

This time Pinocchio prepares himself and then lets out a huge great blast of a whistle. (Probably somebody offstage has to supply this!)

Mr Cricket Cripes! Well done, my boy, well done! (*Beckoning offstage*) Villagers, we've got a genius in our midst—genius with a capital J! Come and join him!

The Villagers and Urchins enter, singing

PRODUCTION NUMBER of SONG 3

They sing one chorus then there is the "Whistling chorus". They stand along the footlights with Mr Cricket and Pinocchio and encourage the Audience to join in and clap time to the music and whistle

Mr Cricket (*calling*) Sensational! Sensational with a capital C!

After the production number and the audience participation, all Chorus exits waving to Pinocchio and making "thumbs up" signs of encouragement. Mr Cricket is the last in the line to exit

(*Posing at the wings, hat held high*) My boy, this could be the beginning of a beautiful relationship!

Mr Cricket exits

Pinocchio (*alone on stage, saying solemnly to himself*) "Be brave and truthful and unselfish, then one day you'll stop being a puppet and become a *real live boy!*"

Gepetto enters with a large spelling book, "ABC" on the cover, but he now has no coat

Gepetto (*handing Pinocchio the book*) Here you are, son! One spelling book!

Act I, Scene 2   17

Pinocchio Hallo, Papa! Hey! Weren't you wearing a coat when you went to the store?
Gepetto No, no, I don't think so . . . no . . .
Pinocchio (*looking inside the book flap*) This cost five lire. You only had two lire. You've exchanged your coat for this book!
Gepetto No, of course not, my boy . . .
Pinocchio You did that for me. I don't know what to say.

Mr Cricket enters

Mr Cricket Say, thank you, you twit!

Mr Cricket exits again

Pinocchio (*seriously*) Thank you, you twit.
Gepetto What?
Pinocchio (*unaware*) Thank you, Papa.
Gepetto And you promise to go to school like a good boy?
Pinocchio Oh *yes*!

Gepetto closes the shop shutters or slides the "shutter front" on from the wings so that it hides the shop interior

Gepetto And now you must get to school and I must get to work!

Gepetto and Pinocchio wave happily to each other

  Gepetto exits into the now closed shop or into the wings

Pinocchio lifts his head up and marches with determination towards the school door

Pinocchio (*as he goes*) School! I'm going to school just like Papa said! (*Chanting quickly*) One, two, three, four, off I go to the school-house door!

He has reached the door but hears the loud boom of a drum beating offstage, so he turns away from the school and watches, intrigued by the drum noise and the beginning of the Puppet Show sequence. The cut-out of the florid proscenium with practical curtains is being flown in or pushed on

  Mr Fire Eater enters beating the big drum

The Schoolchildren are now urchins and they enter excitedly, bringing on benches. The Adult Villagers also enter and noisily sit on the benches and wait for the show to start

Scene 2

The Travelling Puppet Show

Downstage Lampwick enters, stealthily, from the school door and meets Pinocchio

The Juveniles and Villagers enter, while the following lines are spoken

Lampwick (*greatly excited*) The puppet show! It's stupendous!

Pinocchio (*pointing to the school door*) But *school*!
Lampwick (*dragging Pinocchio away from the school area*) School—Pooh! The puppets are great! Almost real! The curtain goes up and everyone claps and it's better than school any day!

Mr Fire Eater puts the big drum on the ground

Lampwick drags the uncertain Pinocchio to where they both sit as part of the excited village audience. We see clearly that Pinocchio is fascinated by the evil and theatrical Mr Fire Eater—he points to him and nudges Lampwick

Mr Fire Eater (*beating the big drum; laughing evilly*) Ha, Come one, come all! Ladies and gentlemen, I am Mr Fire Eater the Puppet Showman so get ready to be astonished, startled and stupefied! Soon you will be seeing my ingenious and incredible puppet show—roll up, roll up!
Pinocchio Incredible! But I *must* be off to school!

Pinocchio starts to go towards the school door but Mr Fire Eater smoothly takes his arm and swings him round, bringing him centre stage

Mr Fire Eater Incredible's the word. (*Flattering the gullible puppet*) And you spoke the word with panache, laddie. You are an *actor*?
Pinocchio Looking at you, I wish I was! It would be *wonderful*!
Mr Fire Eater It *is* wonderful. To be a puppet showman one *must* be an actor! (*He acts a humped back and evil leer*) "Now is the winter of our discontent made glorious summer by this house of York!" (*He ends the line with a ham actor's theatrical gesture*)
Villagers (*applauding*) Bravo! Bravissimo! Bravo!
Mr Fire Eater Ha, ha, ha! Now for the show itself—but first, your ticket money for your superb seats! (*To a Villager*) That will be two lire. (*Threatening*) Well, come on!
Villager (*scared; handing over money after digging in his pocket*) Two lire.
Mr Fire Eater (*collecting money from Lampwick*) Two lire, thank you.
Lampwick (*cockily*) And thank *you*.
Mr Fire Eater (*collecting money*) Some weeks we play in a palace, some weeks we play in a mere village like this. (*As he collects more money, he aggressively asks Pinocchio*) What about paying for *your* ticket, laddie?
Pinocchio Aren't any of them free?
Mr Fire Eater Are you *mad*? Two lire.
Pinocchio (*distressed*) But I haven't got two lire. (*Offering his spelling book*) My father spent the last of his money buying this book for me. It cost two lire *and* his coat, so will you take it in exchange for a seat?
Mr Fire Eater (*taking the proffered book*) I might. (*He examines it doubtfully*) Is it new?
Pinocchio Oh yes, you can see it is! My father Gepetto has just bought it!
Mr Fire Eater (*snarling*) Gepetto! So you're the son of that lazy good for nothing! (*He peers at him*) But you're a *puppet*!
Pinocchio Yes, I am, but one day——
Mr Fire Eater (*putting his hand on Pinocchio's shoulder*) In that case, until Gepetto delivers the puppets I ordered from him, *you* can take their place! (*He laughs evilly*) Ha, ha, ha!

Act I, Scene 2   19

Mr Fire Eater pushes Pinocchio through the centre of the curtains and there is a fanfare

(*To the Village Audience*) Ladies and gentlemen, members of the nobility, village lads and lassies, pray give your undivided attention to my stringed puppets! For now, before your very eyes my puppets will perform a Grand Harlequinade!

The curtains of the small "theatre" open to reveal Harlequin and Columbine, who have elastic attached to their wrists representing their puppet strings, and they dance jerkily

MUSIC 4—Short Dance

After the dance the Villagers applaud. Then the two puppets reprise their dance and as they do, Pinocchio enters the puppet show area and, standing between the two puppets, he joins in their dance reprise. He soon notices their strings, and reacts with angry frowns and head shakings, and he slips the elastic from their wrists. They stop dancing and flop forwards, arms dangling

Mr Fire Eater (*angrily*) Here! What's happening?
Pinocchio (*to the two dangling puppets over the continuous music*) Go on dancing! You can if you try! I can, so you can! Come on—try harder—that's it!

Encouraged by Pinocchio the two puppets attempt to straighten up and dance without strings, soon succeed and are delighted. Pinocchio moves each one forward, well clear of the puppet show area and behind them the elastic strings are left dangling. The Villagers and Mr Fire Eater register astonishment

All No strings!
Pinocchio (*calling out*) One, two, *three*!

On this cue, Pinocchio, Harlequin and Columbine build their dance sequence up into a Production Number

SONG 2 (reprise)

Their greatly energetic song and dance of freedom is soon joined by the astonished Mr Fire Eater, Villagers and Urchins, with everyone dancing like puppets. At the end, the three puppets step forward and bow over and over jerkily, and the Villagers applaud them

Mr Fire Eater No strings!!!
Harlequin
Columbine } (*together, happily bowing*) { Ching boom! Ching boom!
Mr Fire Eater No strings—laddie, I am transfixed by you!

The two puppets stop bowing but Pinocchio continues bobbing up and down

(*Stopping him*) That's enough—that's enough—you're milking it dry!
Pinocchio Are you angry with me?

Mr Fire Eater Angry? No, no, a thousand times no! (*Aside to the Audience*) I'm going to scare the living daylights out of him later. Now we can be billed as the one and only STRINGLESS puppet show! So come, little lad, we have to move on to the next town by nightfall and you must *of course* join us!

Harlequin
Columbine } (*together, nodding their heads*) { Ching boom, ching boom!

Pinocchio (*moving away*) Oh, I couldn't leave my Papa!

Mr Fire Eater Nonsense! You're coming with my troupe!

Harlequin
Columbine } (*together, beckoning to Pinocchio*) { Ching boom! Ching boom!

Pinocchio But I've promised him I'll go to school today—even though I haven't got a spelling book.

Mr Fire Eater (*handing it back with a flourish*) Not only do I give it back to you—but also, I give you *five pieces of money*. That's your salary in advance.

Pinocchio Five lire?

Mr Fire Eater No, no, laddie, five pieces of *gold*! I am paying for your future services, you are coming with me!

Mr Fire Eater hands the coins to Pinocchio, who shows them proudly to Lampwick

Lampwick (*awed*) Mama mia! Five gold pieces!

Pinocchio (*thrilled*) Thank you! But what about the puppets my papa owes you?

Mr Fire Eater My dear little laddie, who wants puppets now? You have taught mine to perform *without strings*! You and I are going to make theatrical history! (*Declaiming with gestures*) "Oh what a rogue and peasant slave am I!"

Pinocchio (*indignantly*) No you're not, I think you're very nice.

Mr Fire Eater "I loved you not—get thee to a nunnery!" (*Theatrically pointing to offstage*)

At this, Pinocchio starts to exit, Mr Fire Eater grabs him and Lampwick and the Villagers laugh

Mr Fire Eater Come back! I'll see you later at the village inn. You're going to be very useful to me! (*Visualizing it*) "Mr Fire Eater's one and only stringless puppet show—*starring Pinocchio!*"

Harlequin
Columbine } (*together*) { Ching boom! Ching boom! So join us!

Pinocchio Yes! I might! (*To Audience*) I won't because I'm scared.

Mr Fire Eater Then that's settled. We leave at midnight. Join us at the old inn and come strolling with us strolling players!

The cut-out proscenium is removed; the village urchins take off the benches and exit together with the Adult Villagers

Mr Fire Eater is preparing to leave

Lampwick See you later, puppet!

Act I, Scene 2   21

> *Lampwick exits, beating the big drum*

Pinocchio See you later!
Mr Fire Eater We start rehearsing tomorrow. In the meantime, remember this, laddie. (*Acting flamboyantly*) "All the world's a stage and all the men and women merely players". (*To Audience*) That's from Gilbert and Sullivan—oh yes it is!
Audience Oh not it isn't!
Mr Fire Eater Then what is it from?
Audience Shakespeare.
Mr Fire Eater Shakespeare? Rubbish! You're nothing but an ignorant shower! (*He laughs evilly*) Ha, ha, ha!

> *With a last gesture and swirl of his cape Mr Fire Eater exits to dramatic chords*

> *Pinocchio stands centre of the stage, looking at the money ecstatically and holding his spelling book*

Pinocchio Yes! Perhaps I *will* join the Puppet Show! But first, *five gold pieces for my papa!*

> *Upstage the Fairy enters with Mr Cricket and they watch proudly as Pinocchio speaks*

I must be brave and truthful and unselfish! First Papa and then—one, two, three, four, off I go to the schoolhouse door!

> *The Fairy and Mr Cricket are delighted so they shake hands then exit*

> *Pinocchio strides towards the puppet shop with much determination*

Pinocchio (*calling*) Papa! Guess what I've got for you, Papa!

> *Mr Fox and Mr Cat enter to dramatic chords that sound spooky*

> *Mr Fox craftily slithers between Pinocchio and the shop*

> *When speaking Mr Cat has a habit of repeating the last few words of Mr Fox's speech and both laugh in a sniggering way. Note: sometimes it is "Miss Cat"*

Mr Fox And just what *have* you got for Papa?
Mr Cat Got for Papa?
Pinocchio Excuse me, I must go in.
Mr Fox But why?
Mr Cat Why? (*Like a meeow*) Why, why, *why*?
Pinocchio Because I've got five gold pieces—look—and I want to give them to him. He'll be so pleased!

> *The two villains exchange glances*

Mr Fox Only five pieces?
Mr Cat Only five?
Pinocchio Well that's a lot!
Mr Fox Five gold pieces a *lot*?

Mr Cat A lot?
Mr Fox \
Mr Cat / (*together*) { Zuz-zuz—zuz! (*They both snigger in their stylized way at this, right hands in front of mouths*)
Mr Fox Now five THOUSAND gold pieces, that would be something——
Mr Cat Would be something, sssssss ...
Pinocchio Well I've only got five.
Mr Fox Even so, if you've five——
Mr Cat If you've five——
Mr Fox The rest is easy!
Mr Cat Rest is easy!
Mr Fox We know a magic place just near the village where you can make far more money!
Mr Cat Far more money!
Mr Fox (*beckoning*) So come with us! (*He starts to exit*)
Mr Cat (*beckoning*) Come with us! (*He starts to exit*)
Pinocchio (*looking at the ground, confused; deciding to ask the Audience*) You're my friends so I can ask you for advice. Mr Fox and Mr Cat are really nice, so shall I go along with this magic idea?
Audience No!
Pinocchio But it'll make some money for Gepetto and me so *shall* I join them?
Audience No!

The Fox and Cat make gestures at the Audience to make them stop

Mr Fox (*to Audience*) Shut yer traps!
Mr Cat Yer traps!
Pinocchio (*to Mr Fox*) My friends and I don't think the magic idea will work.
Mr Fox But it's the place where five gold pieces become five *thousand* gold pieces!
Mr Cat Five *thousand* gold pieces! Purrrrr!
Pinocchio Why that's a miracle—what's this place called?
Mr Fox The Field of Miracles—what else?
Mr Cat What else?
Pinocchio (*convincing himself*) All right, and I'm doing this for my papa! (*He starts to exit*)

Mr Cricket runs in holding his green walking stick/cane

Mr Cricket (*whispering urgently*) Sssssss!

Pinocchio sees him. The other two don't as they are too busy with the mumbo jumbo actions

Mr Cat and Mr Fox exit

Mr Cricket Stop Pinocchio! You promised you'd go to your father! You promised you'd go to school! You need some knowledge—knowledge with a capital N!
Pinocchio Oh it's you ... I will go to school, but later!

Act I, Scene 3   23

Mr Cricket You can't stay with those two villains—they're crooks! They're going to take you on a Crook's Tour.
Pinocchio They're not. They're my friends—they're going to turn my five pieces into five thousand!
Mr Cricket Pull the other one! They're obviously crooks! (*To the Audience*) Aren't they obviously crooks?
Audience Yes!
Pinocchio Oh no they're not!
Mr Cricket (*pushing his hat forward in vaudeville stance*) Oh—yes—they—are.
Pinocchio Oh no they're not!

The Audience is encouraged to participate until stopped by Mr Cricket's next speech

Mr Cricket You hear what your friends down there say? Don't go with 'em! You hear what your friend up here says? Ditto ditto! I'm your Conscience—I'm *begging* you! (*He grabs Pinocchio's arm and pulls him away from the exit*) Pinocchio, take my advice and——
Pinocchio I'm tired of taking advice. (*Suddenly*) And I'm tired of my Conscience, so *there!*

They reach the far exit and Pinocchio shoves the spelling book on to Mr Cricket and pushes him off stage

Pinocchio runs to centre stage

(*Shouting excitedly*) TO THE FIELD OF MIRACLES!

Black-out

Scene 3

The Field of Miracles

The action is continuous as the front cloth is flown in showing the Field on the clifftops with the Village in the distance (or plain tabs can be used)

Mr Fox and Mr Cat enter and sing and dance very much in character as they point up the greed and craftiness in the lyric of Song 7

SONG 7

Pinocchio enters after the song

Mr Fox (*to Pinocchio*) Talking of Money, welcome to the Field of Miracles (*He makes a grand gesture*)
Mr Cat Field of Miracles! (*He makes the same grand gesture*)
Pinocchio But it looks quite an ordinary field to me!
Mr Fox Ordinary? My friend, this is where your dreams come true and your five pieces become five thousand!
Mr Cat Five thousand!
Pinocchio But how?

The three move centre stage and the lighting dims. There is mysterious music and the two villains make magic gestures as they chant to the audience

Mr Fox You dig a hole——
Mr Cat Dig a hole.
Mr Fox Water it with special water——
Mr Cat Special water.
Mr Fox Put two pinches of salt in it.
Mr Cat In it.
Mr Fox Plant your five gold pieces——
Mr Cat Gold pieces.
Mr Fox Say "Gold, gold, magic foodledeedum".
Mr Cat Foodledeedum!
Mr Fox Then you go to sleep. When you wake up, *there (pointing to the ground)* will be a Tree of Gold growing where you planted the gold pieces. The Tree will be covered in gold pieces for you to pick off like fruit!
Mr Cat Like fruit!
Pinocchio (*in an overawed whisper*) It's magic!
Mr Fox (*nodding mysteriously*) Now I must collect the three magic things that work the miracle. (*He goes to the side of the stage and collects them from the wings*)
Mr Cat (*explaining mysteriously to Audience*) They are a spade, a watering can, and sssssssssome ssssssssalt.

Mr Fox returns and hands to Pinocchio a child's spade, a small watering can and a very big packet marked "salt". Pinocchio kneels down

Mr Fox
Mr Cat (*together*) (*slowly chanting over spooky music*) Dig a hole ... put in your five gold pieces ... water them ... sprinkle them with salt ...

As they chant Pinocchio obeys their instructions. After he has sprinkled the salt, Fox and Cat do magical gestures

Mr Fox
Mr Cat (*together*) Gold, gold, magic foodledeedum ...
Pinocchio Gold, gold, magic foodledeedum ...
Mr Fox
Mr Cat (*together*) Then ... you ... go ... to ... sleep ... sleep ... sleeeeeeeeep ... sleeeeeep ...

Mr Cat slumps and falls asleep standing up. He starts to snore loudly

Mr Fox (*hitting Mr Cat*) Not you, you fool! (*Greasily and sarcastically to Pinocchio*) Sweet dreams of your money tree!
Mr Cat Money tree!

They both creep off and exit, Tom and Jerry style, taking spade, watering can and salt packet with them

Pinocchio yawns, stretches, and lays down to sleep on the ground, the gold pieces "in the hole" behind him

Strange music is heard and, near to Pinocchio, we see a small tree covered in big gold coins start to rise or to appear from the wings. (See scenery notes)

Act I, Scene 4

Pinocchio slowly stands up, arms outstretched to the tree, then with eyes still closed, he lies down to sleep again and the vision fades, the tree sinks down into the ground again or goes slowly into the wings

In the dim light, two figures (Mr Fox and Mr Cat) enter in big black cloaks and floppy hats

Mr Fox Nobody knows who I am because I am crafty as a fox!
Mr Cat As a fox!
Mr Fox (*pointing*) There—the gold pieces!
Mr Cat Pieces—sssssss!

They grab the gold pieces from the ground and start to creep off again

Mr Fox Hah! That'll *fox* him!
Mr Cat Yes—cat-cat-catastrophe!

They both snigger at this and wave back to Pinocchio

Mr Fox Sweet dreams of your money tree!
Mr Cat Money tree!
Mr Fox (*to the Audience*) And don't you dare to shout or wake him!
Mr Cat Or wake him!

Mr Fox and Mr Cat exit

The Audience will now probably shout to wake up Pinocchio

Pinocchio (*to the Audience, delightedly*) Five thousand gold pieces! What's the matter? (*Dismayed*) Where's the money tree? (*He looks at the ground*) My money—where's my money? (*He runs about, scared*)

The Audience will tell the story and "feed" Pinocchio the right lines

(*To the Audience*) Mr Fox and Mr Cat? Did they snatch my money? Which way did they go? This way? (*Pointing in the wrong direction*) That way? (*Pointing in the wrong direction*) That way? (*Pointing in the right direction. Cheekily*) Why didn't you say so in the first place! (*Realizing and shouting*) Help! Police! I'll report the loss of my money and get it back! I'll go to the Police Station—yes, I'll go straightaway to ... THE COURT-ROOM!

Pinocchio exits

Black-out

Scene 4

The Courtroom of the Village Police Station

A simple cut-out of a Courtroom is placed in the permanent set of the Village. Benches are already on for the Jury and one seat and bench are brought on for the Judge. The Jury should be given as much to do as possible in this scene

A small procession enters from upstage. Antonio grandly holding a big hammer, Lampwick with a mace, Mr Fox and Mr Cat and the Villagers and the Village Urchins, now wearing three-cornered hats (the Jury), who at once take up their courtroom places on the benches

Antonio places the hammer, and Mr Lampwick the mace, on the Judge's bench

The Judge enters downstage, with small shuffling paces, eyes downward, and muttering

He shuffles across the stage and exits the other side

The Procession could enter through the Auditorium with the Judge bowing and waving

All (*shouting*) Here, Your Worship!
Mr Fox You should be on the Bench!
Mr Cat On the Bench!

The Judge enters, shuffles up to his bench and bumps into it. The Jury laugh and shout

He turns round and sees the Audience and is delighted. He produces a trick bouquet of flowers from up his sleeve and smells it. The Gilbert and Sullivan introduction music has started and he jigs along the footlights, robes flying, as he sings, with the Jury doing accompanying gestures

SONG 8

(Parody of *The Judge's Song* from "Trial By Jury")

Judge	When I, good friends, was called to the Bar
	I thought I was in for a beano
	I'm afraid I went to quite the wrong bar
	And ordered a bottle of Vino
	I know that it wasn't a very good start
	(An Italian judge should be ritzy)
	But now I've a portrait in oils—very smart—
	Yes, it's me hanging in the Uffizi!

The Judge conducts the Jury, Lampwick, Antonio, Mr Fox and Mr Cat

All	But now he's a portrait in oils—very smart—
	Yes it's hanging in the Uffizi!
Judge	A man with fireworks started a plot
	(I remember his trial was a teaser)
	His fireworks exploded—that's why we have got
	A leaning tower of Pisa.
	Now Rome it is said wasn't built in a day
	And it's full of much double dealing
	The Pope even cut Michaelangelo's pay
	When he'd painted the Sistine ceiling
All	The Pope even cut Michaelangelo's pay
	When he'd painted the Sistine ceiling
Judge	In Venice I judged a case all right

Act I, Scene 4

> And was ever so pleased to be thinking
> That I'd managed to make it watertight
> 'Cos Venice, you know, is sinking.
> But though I've travelled all over this land
> (I've been all the way down and up it)
> The strangest case that has come to hand
> Is this one concerning a puppet.

The Judge conducts everyone

All   The strangest case that has come to hand
       Is the one concerning a puppet.
Judge   Oh now I am a judge!
All   And a good judge too!
Judge   Yes now I am a judge!
All   And a good judge too!
Judge   Though all my law is fudge
       Yet I'll never never budge
       But I'll live and die a judge
All   And a good judge too!

The Judge runs up to his bench, sits and sings scales, sorting out the great stack of papers

Judge Meee! Meee! Meee! (*Singing*) "They call me Mimi."

The Jury boisterously applaud

(*To Antonio*) What is the business of the court?
Antonio Ah.... (*He bends his knees, policeman-style*) There's a complaint about the size of the rates.
Judge Size of the rates? You should see the size of the mace!

The rowdy Jury laugh and cheer

Antonio (*patting the Mace*) It is big, you're right, me lud.
Judge Now, ladies and gentlemen of the Jury, I've had a good think about this first case and I've decided it shall be held in camera.

He picks up a pocket camera from his bench and turns to the Jury

So smile please!
Jury (*smiling*) Cheese!

The camera flashes and everyone laughs loudly

Judge (*banging the hammer*) Silence in Court! I want quiet, I want hush — above all I want peace!
Mr Fox (*to Mr Cat with a nudge*) He wants peace!
Mr Cat (*nodding back, encouraging Mr Fox*) Peace-sssss!

Mr Fox slithers up to the Judge

Mr Fox (*out of the corner of his mouth*) You want peace?
Judge (*surprised*) Yes?

Mr Fox (*whispering, holding up a piece of gold*) Piece ... of ... gold!
Judge (*beaming at Mr Fox as he takes it*) Piece of gold! It'll buy me a seat at the opera!

All the Jury join in with the Judge's singing

    (*Singing a few bars*) "Toreador, thou guards me, Toreador, Toreador..."

Mr Cat (*pleased, rubbing his hands together, and addressing the audience*) Buy him a seat at the opera!

Mr Fox (*to the Judge*) I'm sure it'll come in useful *one fine day*.

Judge (*nodding to him, delighted and singing a few bars*) "One fine day we'll notice, a thread of smoke arising on the sea in the far horizon and then the ship appearing..."

All the Jury romantically sing the aria with him, swaying about in time

Mr Fox (*to the Judge*) Nobody's noticed us!

Judge (*as the Jury hums romantically*) Of course they haven't! (*He furtively pockets the gold piece*) A nod is as good as a wink.

Mr Fox returns to Mr Cat

Mr Fox (*to Mr Cat*) A nod is as good as a wink! (*He makes the "thumbs up" sign to Mr Cat*)

Mr Cat (*pleased*) Good as a wink—meeeeeow! (*He makes the "thumbs up" sign*)

Judge (*banging his hammer*) Call the plaintiff!

Antonio What shall I call him, me lud?

Judge Er... call him at six with a cup of tea.

Antonio I can't, me lud. He's a puppet.

Judge A whattit?

Antonio The prisoner is a puppet. He's made of wood. Yes. (*He bends his knees, policeman-style*)

Judge (*greatly indignant; to Audience*) I've got to try a puppet? I'm mortified. A court of law used not to be like this you know—the dignity has gone—the gravity has flown away. (*Singing*) "Won't you come home, Old Bailey?"

Antonio Here is the prisoner!

Jury The prisoner! Hooray!

Pinocchio enters, wearing big black handcuffs, and stands in the box. He is frightened and looks round at the court

Judge Are you a puppet?

Pinocchio (*proudly*) Yes sir. But I don't need strings to work me!

Judge Neither do I!

The Jury laugh loudly

    What a funny fella. Quite obviously guilty. (*He bangs his hammer. Announcing*) Case number seven, that is "Stealing Money". All right tell me what you've stolen.

Act I, Scene 4

Pinocchio (*dismayed*) I haven't stolen anything! (*He points at Mr Fox and Mr Cat*). They stole it! Oh yes they did!
Mr Fox ⎫ (*together*) ⎧ Oh no they didn't!
Mr Cat ⎭   ⎩
Judge (*with huge charm beamed at Mr Fox and Mr Cat*) Of *course* you haven't stolen it. And thank you for the *peace*, it will pay for a seat at Madam Flutterbye. (*He sings a few bars unaccompanied*) "One fine day we'll notice a thread of smoke ..." Oh how I love that song! I remember one year at the Scala at Milan someone came up to me and said ... (*Suddenly and fiercely to Pinocchio*) Do you plead Guilty or VERY Guilty?
Pinocchio (*scared and bewildered*) Neither! I've lost my money!
Judge Loss of money is a crime.
Pinocchio Oh I *know* it is.
Judge There you are then! And you're the one that's lost the money?
Pinocchio (*vehemently and optimistically*) Yes!
Judge Then everything's as clear as custard. You're guilty.
Pinocchio (*bewildered; shouting*) But I'm innocent, innocent! (*He jumps up*)
Antonio (*grabbing hold of him and jumping on each word*) Temper! Temper!
Mr Fox ⎫ (*together*) ⎧ Temper! Temper!
Mr Cat ⎭   ⎩
Judge and Jury (*waving their arms*) Temper! Temper!
Pinocchio (*shouting*) Where's my papa? I told him to come and help me! Gepetto! Gepetto!

Everyone laughs at Pinocchio

Gepetto runs in—all the Jury applaud and call "Good Old Gepetto!" (etc.)

Gepetto STOP!
Antonio Stop? You can't say "stop" in a court of law!
Gepetto I've just said it!

The Jury laughs

(*He runs across to Pinocchio and embraces him emotionally*) It's all right, Pinocchio, I'll look after you.
Pinocchio Yes Papa!
Gepetto (*to the Judge*) Oh, excuse me, Your Highness.
Judge I'm not "Your Highness". This is an Italian court of law. Try again.
Gepetto Your Holiness?
Judge That's better. Well, you'd better be sworn in.

Gepetto says nothing

Well swear, go on swear!
Gepetto (*embarrassed*) I don't like to.
Judge Go on ... swear!
Gepetto All right then ... Knickers.
Judge (*shocked*) Swear in Italian.

Gepetto Yes me lud, Italian Knickers.

The Jury laugh and cheer

Judge (*calling over the laughter*) Don't encourage him! (*To Gepetto*) I presume you have come to talk about opera?

Gepetto I've come to defend my son! I shall tell the truth, the whole truth and nothing but the truth, even if I have to lie to do it!

Judge Quite right. So what has your son done?

Gepetto (*furiously*) It's not what he's done, it's what THEY'VE done!

He points at Mr Fox and Mr Cat and there is a noisy sensation in court at this gesture

Judge (*indignantly*) You can't talk about my friends like that!

Gepetto But I can! I must! I'm here to fight for Pinocchio! He's nearly but not quite my son!

Judge (*with a puzzled frown at Gepetto*) "Nearly but not quite my son?" Have you ever been up before me?

Gepetto (*innocently*) I don't know Your Holiness, what time do you get up?

Everyone laughs boisterously

Judge (*banging his hammer*) Silence. (*He holds up a document with a seal of exaggerated size*) Here is the evidence.

Gepetto That evidence is false!

Judge False? How dare you use the word false in this court room noted for its Justice—and its Opera!

Gepetto (*impatiently*) All right then, falsetto! It's a tissue of lies!

Judge What!

Gepetto A tissue!

Jury Bless you! (*They cheer*)

Judge (*banging his hammer*) The tenor of this court is out of control. (*To Gepetto*) You're a very odd person. Are you going to plead insanity?

Gepetto (*furiously*) Insanity? Are you mad? I'm going to plead for my son!

Judge You can plead for whom you like but you'll never get anywhere without witnesses. (*He looks around*) Where are your witnesses? (*He looks under his stack of papers*) There must be some witnesses somewhere—there always are. (*He points to one end of the Jury*) Did any of *you* see what happened?

Jury No, me lud!

Judge (*pointing to the other end of the Jury*) Did any of *you* see what happened?

Jury No, me lud!

Gepetto looks at the Judge and points several times at the Audience

Judge (*following his pointing*) Ah! (*Addressing the Audience*) Did any of *you* see what happened?

The Audience is encouraged to say "yes"—the Jury also shout "yes"

Act I, Scene 4	31

Speak up! This is a Court of Law! Any of you see what happened?

Gepetto encourages the Audience

Then is Pinocchio innocent?

Gepetto conducts the Audience in their reply. The Jury also shouts

Are you sure?

The Audience is encouraged to say "yes"

You may be sure but are you certain?

The Audience is conducted by Gepetto

(*Delighted*) Then I will now sum up the case! (*To the Audience*) Your honesty, charm and sex appeal have had their effect on me. I have—as they say in legal parlance—done a U-turn. (*Thunderously to Mr Fox and Mr Cat*) Hand over the lolly!

A Juryman near the Judge holds up a large, brightly coloured lollipop

Not that sort of lolly! (*To Mr Fox and Mr Cat*) Hand over the gold to Pinocchio the puppet!

Mr Fox ⎫ (*together*) ⎧ WHAT?
Mr Cat ⎭   ⎩

Antonio Do as you're told—hand over the gold!
Mr Fox (*bitterly*) You call this Justice?
Mr Cat (*bitterly*) Justice—ssssss?

Mr Fox crosses to Pinocchio and hands over the gold pieces furiously

Judge (*loudly announcing to everyone*) Mr Fox and Mr Cat go to prison—and Pinocchio the puppet is free!

The Judge throws a great pile of papers into the air. Everyone cheers and waves. Antonio takes the handcuffs from Pinocchio and puts Mr Cat's left hand and Mr Fox's right hand into them. The Judge comes downstairs from his desk and joins the laughing Gepetto and Pinocchio downstage

Judge Many congratulations! You and your son must be happy as ... happy as ...

Gepetto ⎫ (*together*) ⎧ Corpus!
Pinocchio ⎭   ⎩

Judge Thank you.
Mr Fox (*calling*) We demand legal aid!
Judge (*calling back*) You won't even get lemonade!
Mr Fox (*pointing to the Judge*) Who does he think he is?
Mr Cat (*pointing to the Judge*) Who does he think he isssss?
Judge (*offended*) I don't *think* he is, I *know* he is. (*He sings a reprise conducting the Jury in their lines*)
      I know he is a judge!
Jury   And a good judge too!
Judge   I know he is a judge!

Jury	And a good judge too!
Judge	Though all my law is fudge
	Yet I'll never never budge
	But I'll live and die a judge
All	AND A GOOD JUDGE TOO!

Now the music is played at a fast tempo, as in Gilbert and Sullivan

> *The Judge lifts his solemn robes and jigs off, followed by everyone else cheering loudly and jigging also, including Antonio with Mr Fox and Mr Cat*

The Courtroom scenery is flown or removed, and we are in the Village Square with Gepetto, Pinocchio and Lampwick remaining

The dialogue continues as the set is changed

Pinocchio Oh Papa, you and your friends saved me from prison! I'll never be naughty again.

Gepetto So promise me you will go to school?

Pinocchio Oh *yes*, Papa. (*Chanting quickly*) One, two, three, four, off I go to the schoolhouse door!

Lampwick (*disgustedly*) School? (*He shakes his head vehemently at Pinocchio*) Never!

Gepetto (*not noticing Lampwick*) You're good lads at heart. You don't really mean to be naughty and cheeky, do you?

Lampwick Oh no, sir, no, sir.

Pinocchio My big toe, sir.

Gepetto There you go again! Mama Mia! (*To the Audience*) I must get back to work but if Pinocchio needs help and I'm not there, you'll help him won't you?

The Audience is encouraged to say "yes"

> (*In a mock Italian accent*) Bene, bene! You are kind! You really nice—a people! (*Sympathetically*) What a pity you have to be English!

Gepetto exits

Lampwick Is he really your father?

Pinocchio Yes!

Lampwick But that's Old Gepetto!

Pinocchio I'm only a puppet now but one day when I learn to be good and kind, I'll be a real boy and he will be my real father. Oh! I've forgotten to give him the five gold pieces!

Lampwick Oh *yes*! You've got five gold pieces! I've never seen a gold piece!

Pinocchio Look!

Pinocchio shows the gold to the greatly impressed Lampwick who holds one piece up, bites it, polishes it, etc.

> *During this examination of the money Antonio marches Mr Fox and Mr Cat across the stage. They are now handcuffed and roped to him*

Act I, Scene 4

At the other side of the stage the Mysterious Coachman enters, carrying a big whip

Coachman (*to Audience*) Ho ho ho! I sound like Father Christmas, don't I, me dears? But he's nice and I'm nasty. (*Sinister*) Very nasty. (*He sees Mr Fox and Mr Cat*) Hallo, me dears! Is it you two going to prison?
Mr Fox ⎱ (*together*) ⎱ Yes!
Mr Cat ⎰ ⎰
Coachman What *again*?

Mr Cat nods

Mr Fox You give us some money and we'll give you some good news.
Mr Cat Good mews—*news.*
Coachman (*doubtfully*) Well I don't know, me dears . . .
Mr Fox (*nodding his head several times towards Pinocchio and Lampwick*) Two likely lads for you!

At this, the bluff Coachman studies the two boys and at once rubs his hands together with relish. Then he points urgently offstage. Antonio wonders what he is pointing at and looks offstage. This gives the Coachman the chance to hold up a bag of money which he then gives to Mr Fox

Antonio shrugs, having noticed nothing offstage, and pushes onwards Mr Fox and Mr Cat who start to exit
Mr Fox (*together*) ⎱ (*turning to the Audience; thoroughly nastily*) Two
Mr Cat ⎰ likely lads—sssss!

Antonio, Mr Fox and Mr Cat exit, waving the money bag

The Coachman stands watching the two boys and plotting sinisterly

Pinocchio (*collecting the gold pieces back from Lampwick*) I must give these to Papa and then I must go to school! (*Chanting*) One, two, three, four, off I go to the schoolhouse——
Lampwick School? School is for babies! You don't want to go to school!
Pinocchio (*vehemently*) You mustn't say that, it's wrong. I *want* to go to school. I want to be a real boy that's why.
Lampwick You're a puppet and you'll always be a puppet!
Pinocchio (*scared at this thought*) No! (*Calling*) Gepetto, Father, some gold for you!

Pinocchio and Lampwick start to cross towards the puppet shop but the Coachman strides across to bar their way

Coachman (*heartily*) Arrr, I don't think there's time for that, young gennulmen! You see, any minute now my coach will be arrivin' to take any youngsters as wants to go to that grand old place they calls Funland!
Pinocchio (*still wanting to reach the puppet shop*) What do you do in Funland? Not that I care.
Coachman Nothin'.
Pinocchio Well, then?

Coachman (*mainly to Audience*) Nothin' 'cept eat sweets, ice cream, candy floss, and liquorice allsorteys. Ride roundabouts, play Cowboys and Indians, whizz round on the helter skelter—anything you wants to do as you thinks is fun, well, you can do it in Funland!
Lampwick Sounds great! (*Persuasively nodding his head*) Doesn't it, Pinocchio?

Pinocchio and Lampwick are intrigued now

Pinocchio There must be a snag to it.
Coachman Would I be tellin' you about somethin' if there were a snag to it?
Lampwick *No school?*
Coachman (*laughing heartily*) 'Course not, me dear!
Lampwick (*tickled pink at the idea*) *Well!*
Coachman That's you booked on the coach then. (*To Pinocchio*) And there's room for just one more, me dear.
Pinocchio No! (*Proudly*) I'm going to give some money to my papa and then I'm going to school!
Coachman Play truant!
Lampwick Babies go to school! Come on, stupid!
Coachman What is Funland for? Fun!
Pinocchio (*greatly tempted*) But if I go to school I'll soon be a real boy!
Coachman This is your last chance, me dear!
Lampwick Woodenhead!
Pinocchio You can *call* me Woodenhead if you like but I'm *not* going to Funland.

The Coachman talks to the excited Lampwick, apparently describing Funland

Mr Cricket runs on unseen by everyone, taps Pinocchio on the shoulder and hands the spelling book to him

Pinocchio (*disappointed*) Oh it's you. (*He reluctantly takes the spelling book*)
Mr Cricket (*angrily*) Yes, it's me. Cease what you're doing—cease with a capital S! I'm your conscience! Don't go to Funland! If you want to succeed you've got to work. That's how the beaver builds his dam, damn it! (*Frustrated*) My message is not getting through!
Pinocchio You've made up my mind for me.
Mr Cricket (*pleased*) Good!
Pinocchio I'm going.
Mr Cricket (*alarmed*) WHAT?

The "vamp" of Song 9 starts

What about your Conscience? What about going to school? What about some Honesty? Honesty with a capital O?

The sound of an approaching coach is heard. The music builds up. The Urchins enter pointing offstage

The Urchins join Pinocchio, Lampwick and the Coachman

(*To the Audience*) I have tried—Lord knows, I *have tried*!

Act I, Scene 4

Mr Cricket exits, shrugging desperately

Song 9 begins, in the style of this story and not as played in an American western. The lighting is sinister. The Coachman watches the children cynically, using the lyric of the song to entice them onto the coach

SONG 9

As the Coachman, Village Urchins, Pinocchio and Lampwick sing, supported by the offstage Villagers, dry ice smoke effects begin

> *The brightly coloured coach enters, coinciding with the last notes of the song, pulled by one or two pantomime-style horses. The horses are covered in stripes and coloured spots, much the same as the coach. The whole affair appears gaudy and unreal — the horses could be "human" if required*

Scene 5

The Funland Coach

The Urchins run up to the coach, pat the horses and climb aboard. They hardly need encouragement from the Coachman who is laughing heartily, but also making sure that everyone gets aboard

"Excitement" vamp music links Song 9 with Song 10

Mr Cricket and the Blue Fairy enter during this vamp music, shaking their heads and registering frustration and great distress

Fairy (*pleading*) Pinocchio!

Pinocchio ignores the Fairy and sings the first eight bars of:

SONG 10

After Pinocchio has sung the eight bars Mr Cricket pleads

Mr Cricket (*pleading*) Lampwick!

But Lampwick ignores him and sings the second eight bars of the song

The Coachman sings to Pinocchio, clearly winning him over with balloons and bags of sweets that he collects from the coach, and Pinocchio is so enthusiastic he drops his big spelling book centre stage

Now everyone (including the offstage Villagers) reprise the chorus. At the end of the song all on stage freeze. The Coachman is now standing up in the coach, his arms held up in the air

Fairy (*anxiously*) Lampwick!
Mr Cricket (*anxiously*) Pinocchio!

The Coachman laughs cruelly, cracks his whip and jumps off the coach. Everyone returns to life as the Music of Song 10 is reprised

> *The Urchins push the coach off, shouting and making a great deal of noise*

The distraught Fairy and Mr Cricket exit

The up-tempo music fades

Gepetto runs on to the empty stage

Gepetto (*calling above the fading bedlam*) Pinocchio! Come back! Come back!

Gepetto sees the spelling book on the floor and sadly picks it up. And at once the music segues into the last bars of the Theme Song. As the emotional Theme Music crashes out the offstage Villagers sing the last eight bars of the Theme Song. The lights fade to a spotlight on Gepetto. He looks at the spelling book, looks offstage and shakes his head pathetically as——

—*the* CURTAIN *falls*

ACT II

Scene 1

Funland and the Funland Circus

The Funland coach is on stage, without its horses, downstage left. Prominent is a decorated cart or stall with carnival hooters and hats etc on it. Centre stage is the gawdy entrance to a circus tent and animal cage (with practical door). There is an exit into the wings from this cage

The Coachman is "jovially" watching the Village Urchins noisily running about wearing comedy hats, blaring hooters. Two of the Urchins wear pirate hats and are fighting a duel with toy swords. The atmosphere is that of a schoolchildren's Paradise

The Adult Villagers are now in pierrot costumes as stall keepers, balloon sellers and fairground people. They wear coloured "domino" masks to convey that there is something strange about Funland—maybe they're Brechtian clowns with white faces. They are laughing and jovially calling out their wares over the introduction music, and handing balloons etc. to the boy and girl Urchins

1st Woman (*shouting*) Balloons! Take a balloon, dear, that's it!
2nd Woman (*shouting*) Funny hats—collect a comical hat—here you are, young lad!
3rd Woman (*shouting*) Here's some streamers! And here, what about this blower? (*She blows it*). What about some earrings? Look!
1st Man (*shouting*) Get your toy swords and pistols here! Cricket bats—tennis rackets!
2nd Man Sweets! Chocolates! Ice creams!

Everyone onstage sings

SONG 12 (Production Number)

During the song Pinocchio and Lampwick enter waving flags and balloons and blowing hooters and eating candy floss, singing the song enthusiastically in their solo section

The routine ends, the children continue to dash about and boisterously play

The Urchins and the Funland People gradually exit during the next few speeches

Coachman (*pointing to the stall*) Want an ice cream, me beauties? Or a pop gun? Or one of them hats there, me dear? (*To Audience*) I've got em!

Lampwick and Pinocchio excitedly run to the stall and put on a fez and a Victorian military hat

Pinocchio I'll take a hat and a hooter!
Lampwick (*waving candy floss*) Candy floss! Oh, this place is better than school isn't it Pinocchio?
Pinocchio (*chanting sarcastically*) One, two, three, four, off I go to the schoolhouse door!

Pinocchio and Lampwick both laugh

Lampwick (*putting on the military hat and saluting*) I'm Garibaldi!
Pinocchio (*laughing and pointing at the hat*) That takes the biscuit! (*He looks round happily*) It's like living your life in a toyshop! (*He jumps in the air*) Wheeee!

Lampwick puts his hand to his head

Lampwick Pinocchio, I don't feel well.
Pinocchio Rubbish! You've been eating too many chocolates!
Lampwick I've only had a hundred and ninety-seven.
Pinocchio Well, then!

They both laugh, then Pinocchio puts his hand to his head

I haven't had any chocs, but I don't feel well now.

The Coachman is watching them carefully and craftily

Coachman (*putting a hand on each boy's shoulder*) You're doin' fine, me hearties! Come and have a ride on the roundabout—you'll feel grand after that!
Pinocchio ⎫
Lampwick ⎬ (*together*) ⎰ All right ...

The three exit one side, the Coachman laughing evilly

The Blue Fairy and Mr Cricket enter the other side, both looking unhappy as they gaze round

Mr Cricket This place is sinister—sinister with a capital C ...
Fairy (*distressed*) We can't look after Pinocchio if he is selfish and naughty. He should be back in the village helping his father. What can we do, Mr Cricket, what can we do?

Mr Cricket creeps away and puts on a comedy hat at the stall and takes a large lollipop

(*Shocked*) Mr Cricket! Don't *you* get under the spell of Funland! I've been a fairy for a long time now and I can spy a wicked spell a mile off. I tell you this Mr Cricket, for all the tents and flags and gaiety, *this place is under a wicked spell.*
Mr Cricket (*meekly putting down the hat and lollipop*) Very sorry, Boss (*To the audience*) I'm crushed—crushed with a capital K.

The Fairy remains indignant at Mr Cricket

Act II, Scene 1

Fairy That lollipop you must ignore
When I've gone you *mustn't* lick it
Oh, I can't trust ANYONE anymore
Not even you Mr Cricket!

The Fairy exits

Pinocchio and Lampwick enter from the opposite side

Mr Cricket runs up to the two boys

Mr Cricket (*anxiously*) Lads—listen to me! This is a warning 'cos I'm worried! Boys who don't help anyone but themselves sometimes get a disease called *Donkey Fever!*
Lampwick (*ridiculing him*) Donkey Fever?!
Pinocchio Go away, Mr Cricket! We're enjoying ourselves! This is Funland!
Lampwick And I'm hot after the ride on the roundabout! (*He takes off his military hat to reveal donkey's ears—attached to his head by a band*)
Pinocchio (*pointing to the ears and laughing*) Donkey Fever—ha, ha, ha!
Mr Cricket I hate having to say this, but how about taking off your *own* hat?

Not caring, Pinocchio does so, and also reveals donkey's ears. Mr Cricket shakes his head sadly

Lampwick (*pointing to the ears and laughing*) Donkey Fever—ha, ha, ha!
Pinocchio (*concerned*) We must go and tell the Coachman about this!

Lampwick and Pinocchio exit agitatedly

Mr Cricket (*calling after them*) Pinocchio, I am your Conscience! I see trouble ahead! There's something pointing at you my boy, and that something is the Fickle Finger of Fate! I can't fully fathom your future, but for friendship's sake follow my thoughts and don't forget about furthering your future with your father! (*He shakes his head and dismally ploughs on*) If you were *with* your father, you'd be all right! But you *aren't* with your father so you're all wrong! Be careful—careful with a capital K! (*He groans and then to the Audience*) Oh dear, oh dear.... Boys. What can you do with 'em? They're impossible! As for girls, they're worse!

Mr Cricket exits

Pinocchio and Lampwick enter from the opposite side, now wearing donkey trousers with tails attached, and black ping-pong balls on their noses

Pinocchio Good! Mr Cricket has gone. (*Giggling to Lampwick*) He's a funny little insect, isn't he?
Lampwick (*laughing, but his laugh starts to alter*) He ha ha haw haw hee eee aw eeee aw ...
Pinocchio You sound like a donkey! You *do!* (*Laughing*) Hee haw heeee haw heee haw!
Lampwick So do you, you silly ass! (*Laughing again*) Hee haw heeee haw heee haw!

Pinocchio (*greatly dismayed*) We're turning into donkeys! (*Calling*) Help me, Mr Cricket! Help me, Papa! I want my Papa! Papa! Papa!
Lampwick Heeee haw!

Pinocchio and Lampwick exit, calling desperately for help

The Coachman enters from the opposite side, in a green spotlight

Coachman Well, me dears, when you been hee-hawing like that for a bit you'll be a little hoarse! Arrr! (*He strides about addressing the Audience*) No wonder they calls me "The Mysterious Coachman". 'Cos what Oi does fer a livin' bain't just drivin' a coach—oh, dear me, no! Oi kidnaps naughty kids to Funland, and turns 'em into donkeys—which is not a pretty sight. Now this takes time, me dears. Fer a while they're a horse what still wears human clothes—they're a clothes horse, you might say! (*Sinister laugh*) Ho, ho, ho!

Pinocchio and Lampwick enter in the completed circus horse costume with false forelegs, stooping as they frisk and canter in

Pinocchio (*with inflections, as though saying something*) Hee haw hee haw hee haw!
Lampwick (*inflecting also*) Hee haw hee haw hee!
Coachman (*cynically amused*) Oi'd loik to help you, 'cos I'm a nice jovial old roly poly, Oi am, but unfortunatelee Oi cannot hear a word you is sayin'!
Both (*appealing desperately*) Hee haw hee haw hee haw hee haw hee haw!
Coachman Oooooo, ever so horsey we are in our speech now, me dears! Not cart horses, nor racing horses, we're more like *circus* horses!

A Funland Person enters, hands the Coachman a whip and exits

Now circus horses loves to trot, don't they, me dears, so see if you can trot while I cracks me whip to encourage you a little bit! (*Everything is said "jovially" and he cracks his whip "jovially"*)

Pinocchio and Lampwick are compelled to trot round grotesquely in a circle

Not bad—*but not good either*. Oi've got an important gennulman coming 'ere to see you, so you've got to do better than that, me dears!

Pinocchio and Lampwick remain trotting in time at centre stage, while the Coachman addresses the Audience. As he is talking they try to creep off one side of the stage but their path is blocked by a masked Funland Person. They attempt to creep off the opposite side but are similarly blocked

Lazy varmints! Mind you, if I whips them horses too 'ard they'll 'ave to go into 'orspital, ho ho ho! Now circus 'orses can either be trained with loving care—or the way I trains 'em. (*He cracks the whip at them*) I soon whips them into shape—instant whip you might say. 'Cos once they've reached a certain standard, they can be *sold to a circus*, you see me dears. (*Seeing their escape attempts*) Trying to escape? Oh you don't want to do that, not when I wants Mr Ringmaster to buy you!

Act II, Scene 1   41

A fanfare is heard

And that's him right now, me dears!

The Ringmaster strides on carrying a short baton

(*Jovially*) Mr Ringmaster! (*Cruelly, to the boys*) UP!

The two boys are forced to rise on hind legs as the Coachman flicks his whip

Ringmaster (*saluting and clicking his heels*) Mr Coachman—two three—salute—two three—sah!

Coachman Oi've got another couple of real bad boys what be real good horses! (*To the boys*) Show your paces to yer new master! Show him a bit of horseplay!

Lampwick trys to pose as though in a circus, but falls over

Upsadaisy! (*He cruelly drags Lampwick to his feet and forces both boys into a circus pose, maybe on a circus tub*)

Ringmaster Bravo, Mr Coachman! Bravo—two—three! (*To Audience*) I can soon lick these two lads hinto shape! I wasn't a Sergeant-Major hin the Sardinian Rifles for nothing!

Coachman (*to Audience*) Oi've brought these two in a coach all the way from the *littlest village in Italy* to the *biggest circus in Italy*. Oi have—as they say—taken them for a ride! Ho, ho, ho!

Ringmaster (*saluting*) Thank you, Mr Coachman—two—three—salute—two three—and I will now take them hover! (*With his right hand he salutes and with his left hand he presents the Coachman with some notes*)

Coachman (*delighted*) Five pounds! Thankee, me dear! (*To the Audience*) This be horse money. You know what they calls five pounds? They calls it a pony! Ho, ho, ho!

The Coachman exits

Ringmaster (*stroking his moustache and speaking mainly to the Audience*) Now, my boyos. Now, my little lads. You needn't worry, I was a Sergeant-Major in the harmy so I'm not a villain. (*He shoves his baton under Pinocchio's chin*) Chin held up at a hangle of ninety degrees to the ground when I'm speakin'! (*He paces about in front of them, very much the Sergeant-Major on drill parade*) I'm Renaldo the Ringmaster, hand if you play fair by me I'll play fair by you.

The two boys droop when they hear their day's routine

You wake at six a.m., you work through till six p.m., then you have a big bag of food, then the show is at height. (*To Lampwick*) Stand up, horse, you're not hin your stable now.

The Ringmaster stops and, in order to talk to the drooping Lampwick, he bends over, and Pinocchio gives him a kick

(*Enraged*) You'll wish you 'adn't done that. I'm a military man, I am. I'm going to put my foot down with a very firm hand.

The Ringmaster goes to swipe Pinocchio with his baton but Pinocchio lifts up his prop legs and uses them like a duelling sword. Lampwick joins in, and there is a scuffle

The Coachman enters quickly

The Boys are overpowered and held by the Coachman while the Ringmaster leers at them

So you'd thought you'd escaped from the worries of the world by coming to Funland—well you hain't. You is working for *me* now, little lads. You is working for Renaldo the Ringmaster—two—three—HUNDER THE BIG TOP!

There is a fanfare and circus music begins

The Ringmaster, the Coachman, Pinocchio and Lampwick exit

The Funland People (now dressed as Circus Folk) enter. We see a clown, an acrobat, a trapeze artist and juggler amongst others

SONG 13 (Production number)

After the production number, there is a fanfare

The Ringmaster enters

Circus style music continues, as all the Circus Folk except Clown and Acrobat exit slowly each side, backwards, in a stylistic way

Ringmaster (*over the music*) Hand now, ladies and gentlemen, for your delight and delectation, for your heducation hand hedification, those two perfect performing ponies, Pinocchio and Lampwick!

To the music reprise, Pinocchio and Lampwick enter with circus frills round their waists and circus plumes on their heads

The Clown and Acrobat run forward with two small gates that the boys are to jump over, two circus tubs that they are to stand on, and paper hoops

Hoop-la!

Pinocchio and Lampwick jump through the hoops which are held by Clown and Acrobat

Has never before seen in this part of Hitaly! Hand again! Hup—two—three!

The boys turn back and jump through the hoops again, then fall in a heap

Hand again! Hand again!

The Ringmaster snarls at the Audience, who start to boo

No wonder you're booing, hit's the most disgraceful act what I've ever seen! (*To Clown and Acrobat*) Come on, you two! *Disgraceful!*

Act II, Scene 1

The Ringmaster storms out followed by the Clown and Acrobat, who leave holding the hoops

Pinocchio Oh Lampwick, what have we done?

Lampwick We've been made fools of.

Pinocchio We've been made donkeys of. (*Emotionally*) Oh, if *only* I hadn't been so selfish. "I must be brave, truthful and unselfish—then I'll become a real boy" ... I'll never become a real boy now. Never, never, never!

Lampwick We're up to our donkey's ears in trouble and there's no one to help us.

Pinocchio (*remembering*) Yes there is! (*He puts fingers to his mouth and delivers the piercing whistle he finally managed to achieve in the Act One whistling moment*)

There is a burst of his vaudeville music and Mr Cricket jumps in and poses

The boys are pawing the air with their right legs, like horses

Mr Cricket (*as cheerful as ever*) Well, what d'you know, it's Pinocchio! (*He laughs*) So you've disguised yourself—you're a wonky donkey! Oh, come on, lads, snap out of it, we're not in a very cheerful mood are we?

Pinocchio Heeee haw heeee haw hee, Mr Cricket!

Mr Cricket (*cheerfully*) Why are you laughing like that, you couple of...! (*At last he notices their tails and ears and is much perturbed*) Well I'll smoke a cigar ... a cigar with a capital S ... You've got yourselves into a right old state, haven't you?

Both boys nod, full of remorse

Well ... let's try you out with a test. If you pass the test I'll help you. (*To Pinocchio*) Are you really and TRULY sorry you forgot all about your father?

Pinocchio (*nodding vehemently*) Oh yes, yes, he haw, he haw!

The Ringmaster enters

Mr Cricket Then I will help you! Have confidence in Cricket! Confidence with a capital K! Put your trust in the old firm! I'm afraid of no one! (*He sees the Ringmaster and his confidence collapses*) Oh dear ...

The Ringmaster crosses the stage, looking savage, and the terrified Mr Cricket hides behind the two boys

Ringmaster You need some food! I'll get you two horses some hay—two three. (*He flicks his baton*) *I've* got the whip hand now! Ha ha ha!

The Ringmaster exits

Mr Cricket pops up

Lampwick You're as scared as we are!

Mr Cricket Me? Scared? Impossible! Haven't you heard the expression "courageous as a cricket"?

Both No.

Mr Cricket Neither have I. (*Heroically*) But we'll escape from the circus somehow!
Pinocchio It's closely guarded.
Mr Cricket Then we'll attack the guards! We'll fight! We'll conquer! We'll——

The Coachman enters, angrily glaring at the audience

Oh, dear ... (*He scuttles behind the boys*)
Coachman Oi be guarding the circus with the Ringmaster, so seen anybody about? Noticed a stoopid little green man, with stoopid little green legs and a stoopid little green face?

Mr Cricket reacts but is far too scared to do anything

Pinocchio ⎫
Lampwick ⎭ (*together*) NO!
Coachman If anybody tries to escape from *this* circus it'll be the high jump for 'em. (*He makes a "slitting throat" gesture*)

The Coachman exits angrily

Mr Cricket comes out of hiding and runs to and fro in panic

Mr Cricket Oh dear. Oh, very dear. Oh, very dear indeed. (*Loudly, with an attempt at confidence*) Now to escape!!!

Mr Cricket, Lampwick and Pinocchio start to creep across the stage. Pinocchio looks up pathetically from his bent double donkey position

Pinocchio (*to the Audience*) Poor Father. He must be sick with worry. I wonder if he's looking for me? Poor Father. ...

The Coachman and the Ringmaster enter unexpectedly, blocking the three's exit

Ringmaster So—two three!
Coachman You thought you'd escape did you, me little darlings?
Mr Cricket Fight! (*He stands still doing nothing*) Fight to the bitter end!
Pinocchio That means you as well, Mr Cricket!
Mr Cricket Oh—yes—yes—of course!

Pinocchio, Lampwick and Mr Cricket start to fight fiercely

Pinocchio (*sentimentally*) Oh I wish I was back home with Father ... (*He then kicks the Coachman hard*)
Coachman Ha ha—OW! (*He hops around on one leg*)
Pinocchio That's made you hopping mad!
Lampwick (*kicking the Ringmaster*) Take that, you villain!
Mr Cricket I'm going to hurt you!
Ringmaster You couldn't hurt a flea!
Mr Cricket (*indignantly*) I *am* a flea.
Coachman You can't hurt us, you're a couple of donkeys—gee up!
Lampwick Take your smarmy hands off me!

Act II, Scene 1   45

Pinocchio Let go!
Coachman You're our prisoners now, me dears!
Ringmaster You're animals—two three—and animals *live in cages!*

The Coachman and the Ringmaster push the struggling boys behind the grille of the cage—dramatic chords as they do

Mr Cricket creeps towards the exit, unnoticed by the Villains

Mr Cricket (*heroically, to the Audience*) If anyone dares say I'm a coward ... (*Unheroically*) I dares say they're right!

Mr Cricket exits right

Coachman The other one's escaped!
Ringmaster Let him. These are the two what must be made to suffer!

The Coachman and the Ringmaster lock the cage door

The Coachman and the Ringmaster exit to dramatic music

The Lights dim to a spotlight on the cage

Pinocchio (*calling out*) Oh Papa! If I hadn't been so selfish I wouldn't be in this mess! I'm sorry! I'm sorry! I'm really truly, honestly, ever so sorry!

There is a burst of glissando music and the Fairy enters, right, pushing a greatly scared Mr Cricket

Fairy Mr Cricket, I'm ashamed of you! You ran away!
Mr Cricket I'm sorry, Boss! Religious reasons!
Fairy Religious reasons?
Mr Cricket I'm a devout coward.
Fairy I'll speak to you later. For the moment we must help Pinocchio. (*Calling, in an echoing voice, with cupped hands*) Gepetto! Signor Gepetto!

There is more fairy music and Gepetto enters stylistically, left, in a trance, and looks out front

The tableau is Gepetto, the cage between them, then the Fairy and Mr Cricket

This following sequence is best if it is lit by a follow spotlight travelling to and fro. Gepetto, the Fairy and Mr Cricket all speak out front during this sequence

Gepetto (*emotionally, not querulously*) Pinocchio! Oh, I do want him back! I know he didn't go to school but I forgive him!
Pinocchio (*calling out in the darkness*) I *did* go to school! I did, I did, I did!
Fairy (*huge disapproval*) Truth, truth, real honest truth
   That's what we fairies prefer
   If you won't tell the honest truth
   Nasty things can occur.

There is a loud chord. A spot lights the cage. Pinocchio turns from the back of the cage, comes to the grille and peers out sideways. He has on a false nose, number one. (See costume notes)

Lampwick Pinocchio—your nose!

Pinocchio (*feeling his false nose; alarmed*) Ooooo-er!

The spotlight moves from the cage and returns to the Fairy and Mr Cricket

Lampwick and Pinocchio exit unseen into the wings for the changing of the nose

Mr Cricket (*despairing to the Audience*) What can I say? What can I do? I'd like to tell all you good people that Pinocchio's as good as you are—but, good people, I would be lying. Pinocchio's a bad lot. Tut, tut, tut and I'll say it again. Tut, tut, tut with a capital Tut.

The Lights fade on him shaking his head mournfully and go up on Gepetto

Gepetto Pinocchio! Oh, I do want him back! I don't care if he *did* break my puppets, I forgive him!

Pinocchio (*calling out in the darkness*) I didn't break his puppets, I didn't, I didn't, I didn't!

Fairy   Truth, truth, real honest truth
              That's what we fairies prefer
              If you won't tell the honest truth
              Nasty things can occur.

There is a loud chord. A spot lights the cage. Pinocchio comes to the grille and turns sideways, he has on false nose, number two

Lampwick Pinocchio—your nose!

Pinocchio (*feeling his false nose, with a louder reaction than before*) Ooooooooooooooo-er!

The spotlight moves from the cage and returns to the Fairy and Mr Cricket

Lampwick and Pinocchio exit unseen as before

Mr Cricket (*despairingly to the Audience*) It was only yesterday when I was feeling very happy, feeling everything and everyone was plu-perfect! But you put your trust in a pal like Pinocchio and before you can say Fairy Liquid—sorry, Boss—he's let you down. (*He shakes his head gloomily*) It would be funny if it wasn't so serious. (*Mournfully*) Serious with a capital C ... (*He shakes his head*)

The Lights fade on him and come up on Gepetto

Gepetto Pinocchio! Oh I do want him back! I know he ate all my spaghetti for dinner but I forgive him!

Pinocchio (*calling out in the darkness*) I didn't eat his spaghetti, I didn't, I didn't, I didn't!

Fairy   Truth, truth, real honest truth
              That's what we fairies prefer
              If you won't tell the honest truth
              Nasty things can occur.

There is a loud chord. A spot lights the cage. Pinocchio comes to the grille and turns sideways. He has on false nose, number three, which is two or three feet long and he probably has to hold it in position

Act II, Scene 1

Lampwick (*flabbergasted*) Pinocchio, your nose!
Pinocchio (*feeling his nose; with a huge reaction this time*) Ooooooooo-er! Ooooooo! (*He starts to cry loudly*) Ooooooo—oooooo!

The Audience can clearly see nose number three as it sticks out from the cage. The spotlight moves from the cage and returns to the Fairy and Mr Cricket

Lampwick and Pinocchio exit unseen into the wings

Mr Cricket (*in despair*) So what can you do? You sing, you dance, you crack a couple of jokes with Pinocchio, and what d'you get back? Nix!
Fairy (*also in despair*) And how do we sum it all up? A nose is a nose is a nose!
Mr Cricket (*in tears, sobbing*) A nose with a very big Capital N!

The Lights fade on them and come up on Gepetto

Gepetto Pinocchio! Oh I do want him back! I do want him back! I do want him back ...

Gepetto exits backwards and stylistically

Pinocchio (*calling out in the darkness*) Yes, a nose is a nose is a nose!
Fairy \
Mr Cricket / (*together*) Hark! (*They each put their hand to their ears and listen*)
Pinocchio (*calling out*) All this has happened because I've been lying! But I'm sorry! I only did it to show off! If I call out the words "I'm sorry" then *someone* may hear and *someone* may forgive me! (*Crying*) I'm such a mess! I'm such a stupid puppet! I only did it to show off and I'm sorry!
Fairy (*optimistically*) Oh, Mr Cricket, he's sorry! So something will happen now!
Mr Cricket (*drily*) Yes, it will—look!
Fairy Oh dear ...

Two masked Funland People enter to percussion beats and stand in front of the cage—they are sinister in white Brechtian masks

The Fairy and Mr Cricket move to the side of the stage

But his forgiveness will give me strength, Mr Cricket, I'm sure it will. (*She waves her wand*)
        I'll help you poor Pinocchio
        And the reason's clear of course
        You've been lying and been selfish
        But now you're full of remorse
        You've only thought about yourself
        And you've landed in the stew
        But now you've said you're sorry
        So here is what I'll do.

The Fairy waves her wand at the two Funland People—TING from percussion—they react, and then with clonking effects they both walk like Zombies, passing downstage of the Fairy and Mr Cricket

The two Funland People exit

Mr Cricket (*watching them exit*) Boss, you have more talent in your magic wand than I have in my little finger.
Fairy Then I'll use my magic wand this way ...

The Fairy waves her wand at the cage—loud percussion and a burst of Fairy music—and Pinocchio and Lampwick push open the grille door, run out from the cage as themselves, no longer donkeys, and pose as though they have just completed a magic trick.

There—that's done the trick!
Pinocchio
Lampwick } (*together, imitating a fanfare* { Tarrar!
Mr Cricket   And now you two must run away——
                       Back to the Village quick!!

NOTE: *It is a good plan to close the tabs here to allow longer time for the scene change into Scene 2 "Road Back to Collodi Village"*

Lampwick (*pointing delightedly at Pinocchio's face*) Your nose has shrunk!
Pinocchio (*looking down delightedly at his puppet costume*) And we're not horses any more! How was it done?
Mr Cricket (*making magical gestures*)
                       Metamorphosis!
                       No longer hosis!
Pinocchio Where do we go?
Fairy   The main gates of the Circus
                       That's what you're aiming for!
                       When you arrive they'll open wide
                       And you'll be free once more!

The Fairy and Mr Cricket point offstage

Lampwick (*calling to the Fairy*) I'm not a horse any more! Thanks missis! You're a doll!

Lampwick and Pinocchio run off

The Fairy cringes at Lampwick's last remark

Mr Cricket (*watching them go with great satisfaction*) Rescued! Oh goody, goody!!
Fairy As for *you*——
Mr Cricket (*startled*) Eh?
Fairy I've been watching events. I thought you were going to FIGHT for Pinocchio. But when the enemy came, *you* went!
Mr Cricket I couldn't help it, Boss. They were bigger than me!
Fairy If you were organized *mentally*, all this need never have happened. You've got to *think* in this life, now haven't you?
Mr Cricket (*dejectedly*) I offer apologies, Boss, and I wish to eat humble pie.

Fairy Oh don't be so gloomy, Mr Cricket! If we ORGANIZE ourselves we *shall* win through in the end!

Mr Cricket (*clicking his fingers*) Yes we will! That's what I like about you, Boss, you're efficient with a capital I!

Fairy (*pleased*) You really think so?

Mr Cricket I know so. (*He coughs then recites and acts out his next speech with passion*)

> Boss, your organizational powers are superior
> They put some new GUTS into my old interior
> And I who can sometimes feel pretty inferior
> Now find I have HOPE, bordering on the hysteria.

Mr Cricket bows. The Fairy smiles as he kisses her hand

Sudden shouts of fury from the offstage Coachman and Ringmaster shatter the mood

Fairy (*with sudden panic*) It's them!

Mr Cricket Help! (*To the Audience*) Once again, my composure's decomposed!

Mr Cricket and the Fairy exit

The Coachman and the Ringmaster enter from the opposite side

Coachman (*pointing to the cage*) So they *have* escaped! Well, me dear, Oi wonder what we ought to do ...

Ringmaster I don't know what we ought to do but I know what we're *going* to do. (*Yelling*) AFTER THEM—TWO THREE—ROUSE THE CAMP! (*He blows a whistle*)

Coachman I'll catch them if it's the last thing I do!

Ringmaster It will be!

A few Funland People stumble on stage in various stages of undress

Coachman (*shouting*) Get 'em before they reach the village!

Ringmaster (*shouting*) Form in line—two—three—AT THE DOUBLE—TWO THREE—!

The Field of Miracles frontcloth, or tabs, come in behind the characters on stage but if possible do this earlier as suggested

Scene 2

The Road Back to Collodi Village

Loud chase music begins

SONG 14 (Music only)

Pinocchio and Lampwick enter to the music and go into stylized "running on the spot" which is accentuated by the strobe lighting

The Ringmaster, blowing his whistle, the Coachman and the Funland People chase the two boys "passing each other" in the strobe lighting. The noisy shouts, arm waving and loud music produce chaos which enables the two boys to escape. The various Baddies keep tripping up and falling, with percussion crashes as they do so

   Pinocchio and Lampwick exit

Black-out

Gentle music plays while the frontcloth is flown

Scene 3

The Village again

Upstage, a somewhat shaky little boat is by the quayside

Gepetto is in his day clothes, huddled up, asleep, by the puppet shop, which is open

Gepetto (*waking with a start*) Oh! I'm so tired and lonely since dear little Pinocchio ran away. And I'm so miserable I can't tell night from morning ... I suppose morning is the one with a clear blue sky, like this one ... (*He looks up and starts*) Well! There's the Morning Star! (*He gets up and addresses the sky*)
>Morning Star up in the blue
>Make my morning wish come true
>I wish, I wish, I wish I may
>Find my son again today.

A few bars of the Theme Song are played

The Fairy and Mr Cricket enter upstage, fingers to lips in a "silence" gesture

(*Desperately addressing the sky*) But the trouble is, where did Pinocchio run away to? Where?
Fairy (*in a loud whisper*) Funland.
Mr Cricket (*in a loud whisper*) With a capital P.H. ...

The Fairy and Mr Cricket continue walking across the stage and exit, unseen by Gepetto

Gepetto (*snapping his fingers*) Funland! (*Mystified*) Whatever made me think of that? Funland is down the coast, across the bay ... (*Mystified that he knows this fact*) And why do I know *that*? (*He shrugs*) I'll ask Antonio if I can borrow his boat. (*Calling*) Antonio! Antonio! (*He runs across to Antonio's house and knocks on the door*)

There is no answer

   (*To the Audience, turning to look at them*) Nobody in.

The door opens, but Gepetto does not see this

   I'll try again.

Gepetto knocks, without looking, and hits Antonio, who has appeared at the door, in the face

Act II, Scene 3

Antonio enters

Antonio (*furiously*) OW! What are you doing?
Gepetto I'm knocking on wood! I'm so excited!
Antonio You're jumping like a jelly, Gepetto. (*He bends his knees policeman-style*)
Gepetto Well, so would you! I heard a voice telling me where Lampwick and Pinocchio are!
Antonio (*still furious*) You punched a policeman in the face! You assaulted him in the course of his du—doooo—doo—(*overjoyed and emotionally*) doooo—do you mean Lampwick and Pinocchio?
Gepetto Yes!
Antonio Then where are they?
Gepetto Down the coast at a place called Funland.
Antonio My Lampwick is the scruffiest, rudist, disobedientist oaf in all Italy (*starting to cry*) but Mama mia, I do miss him! (*He takes off his hat, removes the big cockade from it, dabs his eyes with it, tucks it into the hat band again, still sobbing loudly*)
Gepetto I'm going to rescue them! I'm going to borrow your boat!
Antonio (*stopping sobbing at once*) Borrow my boat? Over my dead body!
Gepetto I'm going to unfurl the pinnacle, straighten the mizzen, loosen the hammocker and sail her!
Antonio You? You couldn't sail an ice cream tub! (*He bends his knees policeman-style*)
Gepetto I could and I will! (*He starts to move up to the boat*)
Antonio If Funland is down the coast, you've got to sail across the bay. And have you remembered what's *in* the bay?
Gepetto (*laughing*) Yes! Sea water! Ha ha ha! And I'm going! I'm going! I'm going!
Antonio THE WHALE.
Gepetto (*panicking*) I'm not going, I'm not going, I'm not going. Oh, Antonio, the whale! (*He recovers his bravado*) I don't care! I'm going! I'll enjoy it! I'll have a whale of a time!
Antonio (*threateningly*) You're not going.
Gepetto I am going.
Antonio You're not.
Gepetto I am.
Antonio You're not.

Antonio threatens, and advances on Gepetto, who retreats to the puppet counter

> My beautiful boat sailed by you? It'd be shipwrecked before getting out of the harbour! I wouldn't dream of letting you——

Gepetto picks up the mallet and hits Antonio on the head, who falls on the floor unconscious

Gepetto Sorry Antonio, I must leave you on your ownio. Besides, I'll be rescuing your Lampwick as well as my Pinocchio!

There are thunder and lightning effects

(*Looking up*) Rain! I'll be drenched! (*Dramatically*) There's the rain, the sea and the whale—but a man must do his duty! (*He turns to go up to the boat*)

Mr Fire Eater enters to a dramatic chord, and bars Gepetto's way

Mr Fire Eater I saw you.
Gepetto (*innocently hiding the mallet behind his back*) Saw what?
Mr Fire Eater (*miming hitting Antonio*) BOM! You banged your friend on the bonce and I'm going to report you to the village policeman unless——
Gepetto (*pointing to the body*) That is the village policeman.
Mr Fire Eater Ay? (*Realizing*) So it is. Then I'll report you to the High Court Judge *unless*——
Gepetto (*scared*) Unless what?

Mr Fire Eater walks towards Gepetto threateningly, and Gepetto retreats across the stage

Mr Fire Eater Unless you hand over Pinocchio, you dolt! He's a puppet *but he's got no strings!* He's going to be the star of my puppet show! This week we play Milan, next week Padua, and then—once I've got Pinocchio the fabulous stringless puppet—we'll play the Vatican! SO WHERE IS PINOCCHIO?
Gepetto In Funland.
Mr Fire Eater Funland? He's escaped from there, so you're lying.
Gepetto (*agitated, dithering, aside to the Audience*) He doesn't believe me! He doesn't believe me! He doesn't—I've got an idea. (*To Mr Fire Eater*) All right, I'll help you with Pinocchio if you'll help me with my friend. I can't leave him out here to get wet.
Mr Fire Eater Why not?
Gepetto He'll go rusty.
Mr Fire Eater What am I supposed to do about it?
Gepetto Well, Mr Fire Eater, I can't carry him into his house. But a fine, strong powerful man like you can.
Mr Fire Eater (*grudgingly*) All right ... (*He bends to lift Antonio*).
Gepetto Just a minute, I must feel his heart. He's got a wonky heart, you see.

Gepetto puts his hand in Antonio's trouser pocket and, unseen by Mr Fire Eater, he pulls out a big key

Mr Fire Eater (*highly suspicious*) Since when was his heart in his trouser pocket?
Gepetto When he sits down. Now lift him up—upsadaisy—that's it, oh you *are* kind to help a poor old man and I can't thank you enough and if it wasn't for my rheumatism I'd——

As Gepetto rambles on Mr Fire Eater lifts up Antonio. Gepetto opens the Police House door, lets Mr Fire Eater and Antonio in, then slams the door and locks it

Act II, Scene 4

Mr Fire Eater (*muffled shouting from offstage*) What are you doing? I am Mr Fire Eater! How dare you! What's happening? You've tricked me!
Gepetto Shout all you like! I'm off to Funland to rescue Pinocchio!

There is thunder and lightning and Wagnerian music as Gepetto runs upstage, gets into the boat, holds the mast and poses dramatically

> Now *my* adventure has begun!
> I'll find Funland—AND FIND MY SON!

Black-out

If the boat is practical, it is drawn off with Gepetto on it. The thunder and lightning effects continue whilst the frontcloth is flown in, or the tabs close

Scene 4

The Seashore near the Village—or "In the sea" (see note on page 77)

The Adult Villagers and Antonio enter during the storm effects. They are wearing comically battered sou'westers that are too big for them, old macintoshes, long scarves, crumpled hats and wellington boots. They carry a rope which they heave to and fro, as in a sea shanty, while they line the footlights and sing, with plenty of comic gestures

SONG 15 (Production Number)

Solo	Gepetto has set out to sea in a boat
All	Oh—don't—blow the man down
Solo	We're wondering whether he'll sink or he'll float
All	Don't let the west wind blow the man down
Solo	Out in the bay he has put up his sail
All	Oh—don't—blow the man down
Solo	He's much too old to get caught in a gale
All	Don't let the west wind blow the man down.

The next verse is sung quietly but continue the comic movements

Solo	Over the water and over the wave
All	Oh—don't—blow the man down
Solo	He mustn't die in a watery grave
All	Don't let the west wind blow the man down.

The next verse is sung double forte

All	There's wind and there's rain
	And there's hiss and there's spray!
	Oh—don't—blow the man down!
	He'll be all right, that's if all of us pray!
	Don't let the west wind blow the man down!

Everyone sings a few linking notes to "Aaaaah" that get them into the more rollicking chorus

All	Gepetto is over the ocean Gepetto is over the sea Gepetto is over the ocean Oh bring back Gepetto to me
	Bring back, bring back Oh bring back Gepetto to me, to me Bring back, bring back, Oh bring back Gepetto to me.
Solo	I've got an incredible notion His age is about ninety-three He'll never survive the commotion So bring back Gepetto to me.
All	Bring back, bring back, *etc.*

The next verse is sung quietly

Solo	Just now as I lay on my pillow Just now as I lay on my bed I thought of the waves and the billows And I dreamt Gepetto was dead
All	Bring back, bring back, *etc*

The next verse is sung double forte

Solo	Gepetto's behaviour is manic He doesn't know what he is at I'm thinking about the Titanic We all know what happened to that!
All	Bring back, bring back Oh bring back Gepetto to me, to me Bring back, oh bring back (*Bar room harmony*) Oh—bring—back—Gepetto—to—me!

After the song they lower the rope to the ground. The sea shanty music and storm effects continue

Pinocchio and Lampwick run on. All cheer!

Lampwick We're back! We've escaped!
Antonio My boy! (*He embraces Lampwick*)
All (*delighted*) It's Pinocchio! It's Lampwick! It's the lads back home!

Lampwick greets everyone with handshakes but the worried Pinocchio looks round for his father

Pinocchio Papa! Papa! Where are you, Papa!
Antonio He hit me on the head and he took my boat—he's looking for you!
Lampwick Gepetto the sailor! What a laugh!
Pinocchio (*pointing offstage*) You mean he's out in the bay?
All Yes!

Act II, Scene 4

Pinocchio (*looking offstage and pointing*) And there he is!

Everyone looks offstage

(*Calling offstage*) Oh Papa, you're very brave! There's the boat! (*Scared*) And what's that?

There is a loud dramatic chord and everyone leans forward together

All (*terrified*) THE WHALE!
Antonio The whale! It's swimming towards the boat! It's *swallowed* the boat!
All (*shattered*) No!
Pinocchio (*heroically*) I must save him! I must! I must save my papa! I'm coming, Papa! *I'll swim out to the whale!*

Pinocchio runs off

Antonio Come back, Pinocchio! It's dangerous! Come back! Oh, what's the use? Nobody listens to me. I'm just the village policeman. (*He does his knees bend policeman-style*)

All the Villagers pick up the rope and sway to and fro with it as they sing the sea shanty

1st Solo	Pinocchio shows great devotion
	He's altered a lot you'll agree
2nd Solo	It makes my heart full of emotion
	So bring back that puppet to me.
All	Bring back, bring back *etc.*

The next verse is sung quietly

3rd Solo	Pinocchio's not a good swimmer
	Although he's as brave as can be
	The outlook gets grimmer and grimmer
	As he tries to swim through the sea
All	Bring back, oh bring back *etc.*

The next verse is sung double forte

1st Solo	We hope that he doesn't get bitten
	The whale has got big teeth, you see
2nd Solo	If all this had happened in Britain
	We're sure he'd have got a V.C.

They sing a stirring few bars of the Welsh National Anthem

All	Whales! Whales! Glorious, glorious whales!
	And—bring—back—that—puppet—to—me!

Black-out. Scene 4 (In the Sea) is the alternative to this Sea Shanty scene—see notes on page 77

Scene 5

Inside the Tremendous Whale

A backcloth representing the inside of the Whale hides the village permanent set. The small boat is as far downstage as possible, behind a groundrow that represents the Whale's tongue. Gepetto is sitting in the boat, fishing with a stick and bit of string, as the Lights come up and drip—drip—drip—drip— sounds are heard, there is dry ice and ripple lighting effects

Gepetto (*gazing round and sighing deeply*) I'm inside the Tremendous Whale! I'm finished, I'm up the spout! I did once read the story of Jonah. It tells you how he got into the whale but it doesn't tell you how he got out! So I'll be in here for ever more, with just some little fishes inside this great big fish!

Gepetto sings, accompanied by three girls in seaweed, or glove puppets

SONG 16

On the last word of the chorus the "three little fishes" rise up and make a burp noise. The small dolphins or fish are three props or glove puppets, manipulated from behind the Whale's tongue groundrow which is about four feet high by the time it reaches the wings, and thus the two manipulators are hidden, and the prop fish or glove puppets sing the chorus with squeaky voices

Gepetto (*after the song*) I am hungry. I'd love a whale meat sandwich. And I do wish Pinocchio was here. I wonder if we'll ever meet again. P'raps we will ... (*Singing sadly*) "Whale meat again, don't know where, don't know when ..."

There is a burst of a few bars of "The Flying Dutchman" or "Fingal's Cave" music and Pinocchio enters, with swimming gestures, moving behind the long groundrow doing clear breast stroke gestures

Pinocchio joins Gepetto in the boat

Gepetto (*overjoyed*) Pinocchio—oh, Pinocchio!
Pinocchio Papa!
Gepetto But how did you get in here?
Pinocchio I swam.
Gepetto But you never learnt to swim! Why didn't you sink?
Pinocchio I'm made of wood.
Gepetto Of course. How silly of me.
Pinocchio (*looking round with determination*) Now we're here we've got to get out! *And fast!*
Gepetto (*distressed*) We'll never get out! We'll stay inside here for ever and ever! (*He starts to sob loudly, but recovers*) I may be inside a whale but I mustn't blubber.
Pinocchio (*taking out a large coloured handkerchief*) Here, Papa, blow!
Gepetto (*starting to sob again*) Now I'm crying because I'm so happy to see you! (*He takes the handkerchief and shivers*) It's cold in here—and—(*He

Act II, Scene 6

sneezes) Excuse me. (*He uses the handkerchief again*) Ah—ah——TIS-HOO! (*He holds up the handkerchief and shows a great big hole in it*)
Pinocchio (*laughing*) You've blown a hole in it! (*Dramatically, realizing*) Why, Papa, if you can blow that hole in the hankie, you can blow against the sail!
Gepetto (*excitedly*) And that way we can blow ourselves out of the whale!
Pinocchio That's right! Try it, Papa!

Gepetto sits in the boat, and blows against the sail

Gepetto Nothing happened.
Pinocchio Try again.
Gepetto (*blowing at the sail*) Still nothing happens. We aren't moving.
Pinocchio You haven't enough puff! (*Despondently*) Oh dear ...
Gepetto I know somebody that's got enough puff! (*Pointing to the Audience*) THEY have!
Pinocchio Oh yes, Papa! (*To the Audience*) Will you blow as hard as you can?

Pinocchio and Gepetto encourage the Audience to blow

Gepetto We're not moving!
Pinocchio Not a sausage. (*Encouraging the Audience*) You'll have to blow harder than that!

The Audience blows and we hear a few chords of music. The boat moves a bit

Pinocchio | (*together*) | Another blow! We're nearly there! Come on!
Gepetto |

The Audience blows. Louder music now and it builds to a triumphant sound as the boat moves off

Pinocchio | (*together*) | (*waving to the Audience*) Thank you! Thank you!
Gepetto | | You've saved our lives! Wonderful! We're away

The boat exits to triumphant music

Black-out

Scene 6

The Seashore again

In front of the tabs or a front cloth, the Village Urchins and Antonio. They are anxiously looking off-stage, wearing waterproof clothes, macs, sou' westers etc.

Antonio (*importantly*) Two people swimming ashore. I must make a note of it. (*He takes out a notebook and pencil, does his "knees bend", and writes*) "At seventeen hundred hours on June the fifteenth two——"
Lampwick (*interrupting*) It's my friend Pinocchio!
Antonio (*overjoyed*) And it's *my* friend Gepetto!

Pinocchio and Gepetto run on

Pinocchio, Lampwick, Gepetto and Antonio embrace each other. Antonio puts away his book

Gepetto—the hero!

Everyone starts to cheer but Gepetto silences them at once

Gepetto No, no, it is *Pinocchio*. *He* saved *me*, he's the hero!
All (*cheering*) Pinocchio the hero! Hooray!

Someone lifts Pinocchio on his shoulder, helped by the Village Urchins, and there is a quick fanfare

The tableau is held whilst everyone applauds Pinocchio. Then he is set down. Pinocchio and Lampwick stand between their respective fathers, swivelling their heads to and fro during the following slanging match

Antonio (*suddenly remembering*) Hey! you bagged my boat! Yes, you did, you stupid cart horse!
Gepetto You ... you ... policeman!
Antonio You ancient mariner!
Gepetto You lousy land lubber!
Antonio You clodhopper!
Gepetto If I'm a clodhopper, you're a hyena!
Antonio Dolt!
Gepetto Dunderhead!
Antonio Ignoramous!
Gepetto Gump!
Antonio Gump? What's a gump?
Gepetto I don't know. I just thought of it.

Pinocchio separates the two fathers

Pinocchio Now I know you're great friends and you want to talk quietly about the adventure, but I'm tired! (*He yawns and stretches*)
Antonio He is right! Pinocchio the hero is right!
All Hooray! Pinocchio the hero!

Gepetto pats Pinocchio's head and places it against his chest, and Pinocchio closes his eyes

Gepetto There, there, Pinocchio, of course you're tired. (*To the others*) Sing him to sleep.

Antonio conducts the Villagers who now sing **Song 17** (*reprise*) *softly*

Solo	Pinocchio rescued his friend from the whale
All	Oh—don't—blow the boy down
Solo	We knew he was brave and that he wouldn't fail
All	Don't let the west wind blow the boy down

They sing the second tune of the Sea Shanty sequence

All	Pinocchio rescued Gepetto
	And all of us here want to say
	The puppet is clearly a hero
	Today is Pinocchio's day

Act II, Scene 7

All (*quietly*) Sleep tight, sleep tight
You brought back Gepetto to me, to me
Sleep tight, good night,
You—brought—back—Gepetto—to—me. ...

The tabs open or the frontcloth is flown

SCENE 7

Collodi Village

On the last note of the song, all say "Ssssh" to each other and with fingers to mouths they creep away and exit at various places round the Village set

NOTE: There is usually ample time for this scene change as all that is needed is Gepetto's shop. If longer time is needed, the Villagers sing a chorus of another sea shanty between the two above sea shanty parodies

As the Villagers exit, the Lights dim, and Gepetto takes from the shop counter his nightcap and gown that he wore at the opening of the play and puts them on as he speaks

Gepetto (*chuckling*) Well, I've heard you called many things, but I never thought I'd hear you called a hero!
Pinocchio Nor me, Papa!
Gepetto You're a *good* Pinocchio, so you can sleep under the counter.
Pinocchio No I'll sleep *on* the counter.
Gepetto I wouldn't dream of it. Take my bed behind the counter. Please. I insist.
Pinocchio All right, Papa. And thank you. (*He goes round behind the counter, stretching, and then sees the ABC spelling book on the counter top*) My spelling book!
Gepetto You left it behind when you went to Funland.
Pinocchio (*holding up the book*) I want to promise you something, Papa.
Gepetto Promise me something? Promise me what?

The offstage cast is heard singing the Theme Song quietly

The Fairy and Mr Cricket enter upstage and listen proudly to Pinocchio with beaming smiles

Pinocchio I want to promise you I'll never be a bad boy again. I'll never break your puppets or eat your spaghetti or run away to Funland again. I'll be a *good* boy and I *will* go to school this time. Yes, tomorrow morning, one, two, three, four, I *will* go to the schoolhouse door!
Gepetto So you have got a conscience after all!

Upstage, the Fairy and Mr Cricket shake hands

(*Pleased*) You have altered, my Pinocchio! You're not only a hero but you want to go to school as well! (*Aside to the Audience*) I still can't believe it. (*He starts to settle down at the front of the counter*)

Pinocchio frowns and concentrates very hard on the spelling book, as the Theme Song continues quietly

Pinocchio Cuck—cuck—cuck—C ... A ... T ... spells cuck ... cuck ... CAT!
Gepetto (*much pleased, emotionally*) Pinocchio!
Pinocchio Dud ... dud ... DOG!
Gepetto Very good!

Pinocchio puts the book down and goes behind the counter and yawns and stretches

Pinocchio (*cockily*) Yes, I'll soon have a University Degree, and then I'll be a Prime Minister and I might be President of Italy—or the King, I haven't decided yet.
Gepetto (*laughing*) Still the same old Pinocchio!

Pinocchio's next speech is the last dialogue spoken as a puppet, so it should be very much in his high pitched puppety voice

Pinocchio Good-night, Papa (*He disappears down behind the counter*)
Gepetto Good-night, son. (*He settles down by the front of the counter and falls asleep*)

Pinocchio exits unseen for his costume change

The Fairy and Mr Cricket move downstage

Fairy (*triumphantly*) At last! Victory!
Mr Cricket Triumph! Spelt with a T as in Brooke Bond!

A loud music chord clangs out for the song introduction and they sing together, as a victorious team

SONG 19

They both end the song double forte, make a big vaudeville exit

At once the Theme Song is played

The Fairy enters to re-enact a fast version of the opening moments of the play

The Fairy points to the school and the school bell is heard. She swirls across and taps Antonio's door with her wand

The Fairy exits

Antonio enters, struggling into his coat and hat

The Schoolchildren run on with their ABC books

The Adult Villagers enter, wearing the costume of the first scene

Antonio (*blustering, loudly*) Lampwick, time for school! The bell's ringing! My son Lampwick is the laziest boy in the village and——

Lampwick rushes out with neat appearance and stands to attention and salutes

Act II, Scene 7

Lampwick Ready, Papa!
Antonio (*gasping in comic amazement*) I can't believe it! Kiss your father.
Lampwick (*pulling a face*) Eeuuuuuuuuurch. (*Remembering himself*) Yes, Papa! (*He kisses Antonio dutifully*)
Antonio And we must wake up your school friend—it's his first day at school!

Gepetto wakes up, stands up, and begins taking off his night gown

Gepetto Yes, now that Pinocchio is brave and honest and good, p'raps he *will* go to school! I'll try him out. (*Calling*) Wake up, Pinocchio!

All on stage freeze and turn their backs to the Audience

From each side the Fairy and Mr Cricket enter downstage, point to the Puppet shop and also freeze

The first few bars of the Theme Song are reprised loudly and dramatically, then stop. Silence

Pinocchio stands up from behind the counter and steps forward. He is an elegant and well dressed schoolboy with exceedingly smart cap and suit. All the puppet paint on his face has gone, so has his eccentric clothing

Gepetto (*gasping*) You're a real boy!
Pinocchio (*using a non-puppety voice for the first time*) Oh, Papa! I can't believe it! I'm a real boy. (*To the Audience, running to and fro excitedly*) I'm a real boy! I'm a real boy! I'm a real boy!

Pinocchio and Gepetto embrace with tremendous happiness. Everyone on stage turns to the Audience and sings the last eight bars of the Theme Song

SONG 20

The CURTAIN *falls, then rises again*

SONG 21 (Finale)

Reprises of the main up tempo songs to get the Audience to clap in time as everyone takes their bows. Then all sing the last bars of The Theme Song as Gepetto and Pinocchio take their bows, and into the finale couplets

Mr Cricket	That's the end of the show!
Gepetto	There's nothing more to see!
Pinocchio	So goodbye from Pinocchio!
Everybody	Pinocchio with a capital P!!

Final Chorus

CURTAIN

FURNITURE AND PROPERTY LIST

See note on permanent set, and other settings, which follow this list

ACT I

Scene 1

On stage: Permanent set
In Gepetto's shop: Puppets (including one good puppet), coloured scarf, paintbrush, paint, mattress (optional) in front of counter, coloured coat on a hook. Shop counter. *On it:* puppet, mallet, chisel, "nails", oil can, plate, knife, fork. *Behind counter:* knife, bedraggled puppet, plastic bag for spaghetti.

Off stage: Notice—I AM NOT IN **(in Police Station)**
Log (see scenery note)
Plate of spaghetti **(Pinocchio)**
ABC book **(Gepetto)**

Personal: **Fairy:** wand
Schoolchildren: each has an ABC book
Mr Cricket: walking stick
Lampwick: ABC spelling book, catapult
Mr Fire Eater: badly made puppet doll
Gepetto: 2 lire coin

Scene 2

On stage: Permanent set with puppet show proscenium

Off stage: Benches **(Urchins)**

Personal: **Mr Fire Eater:** Big drum

Scene 3

On stage: Field of Miracles frontcloth

Off stage: Spade, watering can, salt **(Mr Fox and Mr Cat)**

Personal: **Mr Fox:** Cloak, hat
Mr Cat: Cloak, hat

Scene 4

On stage: Permanent set with Courtroom setting

Set: Benches on stage. Judge's bench. *On it:* camera (practical), document with seal, stack of papers. Witness box (cut-out)

Pinocchio

Off stage: Hammer **(Antonio)**
Mace **(Lampwick)**
Spelling book **(Mr Cricket)**

Personal: **Villagers:** Three cornered hats (as Jury)
Pinocchio: Handcuffs (large prop ones)
Juryman: Lollipop
Coachman: Whip, bag of money

Scene 5

On stage: Permanent set with Funland Coach

Off stage: Funland Coach. *In it:* sweets, balloons, etc.

ACT II

Scene 1

On stage: Funland Coach (without horses)
Fairground stalls. *On them:* Hats (including two large ones—a fez and a military one), balloons, candy floss, lollipops, etc.
Circus tent and animal cage entrance
Circus tubs
Two small gates (optional)
Paper hoops

Off stage: Whip **(Funland person)**
Various stages of donkey costumes **(Pinocchio and Lampwick)**
Nose in various stages **(Pinocchio)**
Frills and plumes **(Pinocchio and Lampwick)**

Personal: **Urchins:** hats, balloons, toy swords
Funland People: Balloons, hats, sweets, etc. Domino masks
Ringmaster: Baton, money, whistle

Scene 2

On stage: Frontcloth

Scene 3

On stage: Permanent set

Set: Mallet on shop counter

Personal: **Antonio:** Key

Scene 4

On stage: Permanent set

Scene 5

On stage: Cloth for Tremendous Whale

Off stage: Three glove puppets **(Stage Management)**

Personal: **Gepetto:** Stock, piece of string
Pinocchio: handkerchief with hole in it

SCENE 6

On stage: Permanent set

Personal: **Antonio:** Notebook, pencil

SCENE 7

On stage: Permanent set

Set: **Gepetto's** nightgown and cap and ABC spelling book on counter

Off stage: Spelling books **(Schoolchildren)**

LIGHTING PLOT

Only essential cues are given. Other lighting effects may be added at the Director's discretion

Property fittings required: nil

Several exterior and one interior settings: permanent village set with frontcloths

ACT I, SCENE 1

To open: dim lighting

Cue 1	**Fairy** waves her wand *Gradual fade up to sunlight*	(Page 1)
Cue 2	**Mr Fire Eater** *Green spotlight on Mr Fire Eater*	(Page 2)
Cue 3	**Pinocchio** runs into Auditorium *House lights up*	(Page 10)
Cue 4	**Pinocchio** runs back on stage *House lights off*	(Page 10)
Cue 5	**Mr Cricket:** "That I like to do!" *Lights down to spotlight on Mr Cricket*	(Page 15)
Cue 6	**Mr Cricket** exits *Fade spotlight and revert to sunlight effect*	(Page 16)

ACT I, SCENE 2

To open: full lighting

| Cue 7 | **Pinocchio:** "... FIELD OF MIRACLES!"
Black-out | (Page 23) |

ACT I, SCENE 3

To open: full lighting

| Cue 8 | **Pinocchio:** "But how?"
Lights dim | (Page 23) |
| Cue 9 | **Pinocchio:** "THE COURTROOM!"
Black-out | (Page 25) |

ACT I, SCENE 4

To open: full lighting

Cue 10	As Song 9 begins *Sinister lighting*	(Page 35)

ACT I, SCENE 5

To open: continue sinister lighting to end of Act I

Cue 11	After offstage Villagers have reprised Song 2 *Single spots on Gepetto*	(Page 36)

ACT II, SCENE 1

To open: full lighting

Cue 12	**The Coachman** enters *Green spotlight*	(Page 40)
Cue 13	**Coachman** and **Ringmaster** lock boys in the cage *Dim to faint spot on cage*	(Page 45)
Cue 14	**Fairy** and **Mr Cricket** enter *Follow spots on both characters*	(Page 45)
Cue 15	**Gepetto** enters *Follow spot on Gepetto*	(Page 45)

N.B. Refer to script during next sequence for travelling spot cues

ACT II, SCENE 2

To open: full lighting

Cue 16	Song 14 starts *Black-out for strobe lighting in front of tabs or frontcloth*	(Page 49)
Cue 17	**Pinocchio** and **Lampwick** exit after chase *Blackout*	(Page 50)

ACT II, SCENE 3

To open: full lighting

Cue 18	**Gepetto**: "... as well as my Pinocchio!" *Lightning*	(Page 51)
Cue 19	**Gepetto**: "... to rescue Pinocchio!" *Lightning*	(Page 53)
Cue 20	**Gepetto**: "AND ... FIND MY SON!" *Black-out*	(Page 53)

ACT II, SCENE 4

To open: storm lighting, with lightning

Cue 21	As SCENE 4 begins *Lightning, continuing throughout scene*	(Page 53)

Cue 22	**All** (singing): "That-puppet-to-me!" *Black-out*	(Page 55)

ACT II, SCENE 5

To open: dim lighting, with ripple effects

Cue 23	The boat exits *Black-out*	(Page 57)

ACT II, SCENE 6

To open: brighter, after-storm lighting

No cues

ACT II, SCENE 7

To open: full lighting

Cue 24	**Gepetto** puts on his nightgown *Lights dim*	(Page 59)
Cue 25	As school bell is rung *Gradual fade up to sunlight*	(Page 60)

EFFECTS PLOT

ACT I

Cue 1	**Fairy** waves her wand at school *School bell rings*	(Page 1)
Cue 2	**Children** laugh at Lampwick *School bell stops*	(Page 1)
Cue 3	As **Mr Fire Eater** enters *Thunder and lightning effects*	(Page 2)
Cue 4	**Mr Fire Eater** waves the puppet threateningly *Thunder and lightning effects. Dramatic chords*	(Page 3)
Cue 5	**Gepetto:** "... I'd starve!" *School bell rings*	(Page 3)
Cue 6	**Gepetto** holds chisel up *Flash in footlights*	(Page 7)
Cue 7	**Gepetto:** "... not just a puppet!" *Drum beat*	(Page 11)
Cue 8	As **Mr Fire Eater** enters *Fanfare. Thunder and lightning. Dramatic chords*	(Page 11)
Cue 9	**Pinocchio** reaches the school door *Drum beat*	(Page 17)
Cue 10	**Mr Fire Eater** pushes **Pinocchio** through the curtain *Fanfare*	(Page 19)
Cue 11	**Pinocchio:** "But how?" *Mysterious music*	(Page 23)
Cue 12	**Pinocchio** sleeps *Strange music*	(Page 24)
Cue 13	**Mr Cricket:** "... with a capital O?" *Coach effects*	(Page 34)
Cue 14	At beginning of Song 9 *Dry ice effects*	(Page 35)

ACT II

Cue 15	**Coachman:** "... Mr Ringmaster to buy you." *Fanfare*	(Page 41)
Cue 16	**Mr Ringmaster:** "HUNDER THE BIG TOP!" *Fanfare*	(Page 42)

Cue 17	After Song 13 *Fanfare*	(Page 42)
Cue 18	**Gepetto:** "... as well as my Pinocchio!" *Thunder*	(Page 51)
Cue 19	**Gepetto:** "... to rescue Pinocchio!" *Thunder*	(Page 53)
Cue 20	As SCENE 4 begins *Storm effects—continue through scene*	(Page 53)
Cue 21	As SCENE 5 starts *Drip, drip, drip effects, plus dry ice*	(Page 56)
Cue 22	As **Pinocchio** is lifted shoulder high *Fanfare*	(Page 58)
Cue 23	**Fairy** points to school *School bell rings*	(Page 60)

SCENERY SUGGESTIONS

In the various productions I have seen, the following has been the arrangement.

The Permanent Set. Down left is a wing with a door that is the Police Station with "Police" written above. Upstage is the rostrum representing a quayside and behind it a practical small boat with mast and flimsy sail. Upstage right is Gepetto's puppet shop touching the wings. Downstage right, balancing the Police Station, is the wing with a door and a School sign above. The doors of the Police Station and School were practical but need not be—the cast can exit behind the wing and the doors be merely painted on the wings. The Village is "story book" Italian in style.

Gepetto's Shop is a kiosk or can be just a counter behind which is a flat to look like a wall with many puppets hanging untidily. A simple cut-out of shop shutters is needed to sometimes hide the shop interior, and can be moved on from the wings. Ensure that the shop has an unseen exit into the wings which is easily done if the shop is touching the wings.

The Magic Log is held upside down by Gepetto and Antonio who mime that it is heavy. It is similar to a six-foot-long window box with no ends to it and is best made in conjunction with the person playing Pinocchio. Either a wire frame with canvas over, looking like a yuletide log, or hardboard tacked on to a light wooden frame. Either way it should be painted brown with clear grain markings. It is placed on the floor by the wings and because it has no ends, Pinocchio can be slid into it without the audience seeing. At the correct moment the log is drawn "magically" off into the wings, leaving Pinocchio lying on stage where all can now see him.

Mr Fire Eater's Puppet Show. The florid proscenium of the puppet show is a cut out that can be brought onstage by the Villagers. It has practical curtains of lightweight material and is eight or nine foot high. At the same time, other Villagers bring on the backing which is florid Harlequinade scenery, though this idea is not essential and we could see straight through to the upstage village set which is in darkness. What *is* essential is that the audience must be able to see the strings for the two puppets. To each side of the top of the back of the proscenium there are attached two pieces of thick elastic with loops on the ends through which the puppets put their wrists. The curtains to the puppet show draw up to the corners of the proscenium and do not draw open on rails and thus they do not get in the way of the elastic "puppet strings". The proscenium can be held steady by a Villager at each side who, in view of the Audience, can arrange French braces and stage weights to stand the proscenium upright. If you have no wing space close the tabs when Mr Fire Eater enters with his drum and play the scene in front of tabs until the easily erected puppet show proscenium is set, and then open the tabs during Song 5.

The Field of Miracles is the only frontcloth and is a field (with furrows) on the cliff top so that we can see the sea, and in the distance Collodi Village. This scene can be played in front of tabs.

The Money Tree is Pinocchio's dream. It is a cut-out slowly pushed on in front of the tabs or frontcloth. Sometimes it is flown in, like a sort of chandelier. It could light up, then the lights fade as it is pulled offstage when the short dream ends.

Or, if the tabs are used for The Field of Miracles, then open them to reveal a six feet wide flat that suggests bushes and a groundrow of ferns and rocks. The five-feet-high canvas tree rises up from this groundrow and must then slowly sink "into the ground" again so let a stage hand stand behind the tabs at the *side* of the flat and use a stick—a broom handle is ideal. As he raises then lowers this stick attached to the top of the canvas Money Tree it grows and then sinks again. The big sparkling gold coins are clearly seen as though fruit on the tree.

The Courtroom need only be a cut-out of a comedy coat of arms above the Judge's Bench (practical) and a witness box (practical). School benches are used for the Villagers to watch the puppet show and for the Jury to sit on in this Courtroom scene. The Judge being centre stage, the witness box stage right, the Jury benches stage left and we can probably see some of the Village permanent set. Give the Jury as much movement and noise as possible.

The Funland Coach enters pulled on by one or two "panto horse"-style donkeys and should be gaudy and attractive. It could be almost a cut-out because although you may like a couple of Urchins to climb on it, this isn't essential. It is important that it looks fun with floating gas balloons and streamers attached to it.

Funland is a cloth or cut-out showing a gaudy entrance to a circus with the word "CIRCUS" written above in fairground lettering, and next to it is a grim looking cage with practical door and an unseen exit into the wings. This cloth hides the Village permanent set.

The Little Boat is either a box on wheels, pulled off by a rope or (where there is no wing space) it can be a cut-out that is easily manipulated by Gepetto. There is a mast and flimsy sail and the height of the actual body of the boat is about three feet, so that we can see the boat above the quayside rostrum and later, above the groundrow that represents the Whale's tongue.

The Seashore is the same as The Field of Miracles frontcloth or is in front of tabs. But you may well prefer Act II Scene 4 to be "In the Sea".

In the Sea. In front of tabs or preferably a black or dark coloured frontcloth, two girls (in dark clothes or ponchos over their costumes) enter. The one girl crosses the stage quickly and they then hold up a cloth that is the same length as the width of the stage's opening, and its depth is about three foot six inches. Sometimes this cloth has been partly treated with fluorescent paint and of course the following cut-outs need to be painted in this way. These cut-outs are carried by the Chorus, each in turn crossing the stage behind the blue cloth held up. Make sure that there is "Pace", and that the stage is never empty. This U.V. scene is easy to evolve yet looks excellent. The cut-outs are, for example: A dolphin, crab, sea horse, a shark with massive teeth in its open mouth, a human skeleton (easily painted on black material or hardwood) a whale that may need two "holders", a sea anemone. These are all cut-outs held up on black poles and moved up and down—as though swimming—by the holders. A black umbrella that is made to revolve by the holder. It has a jelly fish painted in fluorescent paint attached to it. The same idea for a star fish that crosses later. A quite big square of black cloth is held up by two holders and on this are attached a shoal of about six smaller fish, all facing the same way, that appear to be swimming in a group, especially when the cloth is billowed. A cut-out of a Walt Disney style octopus with big eyes and tentacles that can easily be made to move by a second "holder". On two black poles, held by two people, is a very long eel that wriggles up and down as the black poles that support it are raised and lowered. The routine ends with whatever is your most spectacular item—the whale, or maybe the big octopus followed by its "daughter", a much smaller octopus. After the routine, BLACK-OUT. The front tabs or dark frontcloth or "blacks" is removed, the two girls (holding up the cloth representing the sea) exit, and we are into SCENE 5, "Inside the Tremendous Whale".

Inside The Tremendous Whale is represented by a cloth or a big cut-out painted in arched perspectives as the roof of the Whale's mouth and the ribs of its stomach. (This cloth hides the Village set.) As far downstage as possible is the groundrow of the Whale's tongue, behind which is the little boat. If a small production, use a cut-out of the Whale's wide open mouth and through this can be seen the little boat, and there is either some backing to hide the Village or the upstage area is unlit. The set and the groundrow should be painted a warm red colour to suggest the fleshy inside of the Whale's mouth and stomach.

A Production In The Round can be staged by using a permanent set of the Village and various cut-outs brought on in a sylized way in full view of the Audience, in front of the permanent set, to represent the various other scenes. The story is well suited to a stylized treatment such as this.

You may be using your own choice of music but if so please be sure to use up-tempo and breezy songs, and make the Blue Fairy a brisk lady. Let the gutsy hornpipe song sung by the daft villagers in Act II have zany comedy movements and choreography as well as the "rope-pulling"—make it almost a Keystone Cops style scene when they sing.

J.M.

COSTUME SUGGESTIONS

There are some good illustrated books in public libraries but the following ideas may help.

No costume changes are required except for the Chorus of Villagers and Juveniles.

Pinocchio's costume and make-up clearly show he is a puppet. His bright-coloured coat has over-large buttons and over-large bow tie. His tights are painted to look like grained wooden legs. He has either a zany rag doll wig or a pixie-style hat. His make-up is big eyes and a big red blob (don't use yellow or orange blobs) on each cheek. All trace of puppet make-up and clothes are removed for the final scene when he enters as a "good and hardworking real schoolboy" in immaculate clothes—a very clear costume change indeed.

Gepetto wears an apron and brown baggy breeches and crumpled white stockings. He has white or grey side whiskers and hair, and a droopy moustache. He wears spectacles on the end of his nose.

Mr Cricket is however you think a human-sized cricket should look! If the actor or actress plays him 1900 cockney music hall style then dress him entirely in green with green face and green cockney cap that has two antennae sticking out of it. (Made of wire bound with green tape with a green pom-pom on the end of each antenna.) Or a more posh sort of music hall artiste with green bowler or top hat (plus antennae), green face, green big flowing bow tie, green frock coat, green tight trousers and big boots. A green walking stick helps him to pose stylistically and green gloves save hand make-up.

Antonio wears the Napoleonic-style Italian 1900 Policeman's coat and cockade hat. When his coat is removed he wears a bright red shirt and carpenter's apron. Red nose, red hair, red shirt—all in contrast to Gepetto.

Lampwick wears untidy schoolboy clothes of 1900, something like Oliver Twist looks when he is no longer poor.

The Blue Fairy moves about a good deal, with gliding motions so some lightweight blue flowing dress to the floor is right. A big fantastical blue wig with sequin glitter effects, and a blue wand with a blue star at its end.

Mr Fire Eater wears evening tails, an opera cloak, opera hat and white gloves but should not be costumed too much for reality, and a big flowing bow tie and coloured cloak would help. He must look menacing, like Svengali, with red make up round the eyes so that his appearance goes with his name. He could also have pointed eyebrows, or perhaps a beard, so that he appears almost "unreal".

Mr Fox is a 1900 dandy in Norfolk jacket and knickerbockers with a fox's bushy tail hanging down. He wears a mask which stops just below the fox's nose so that his voice can be heard.

Mr Cat also wears a mask and his suit is black or orange with a cat's tail sticking out. Sometimes Mr Cat is dressed as a period burglar.

The Mysterious Coachman wears Dickensian coachman clothes and carries a bull whip.

The Circus Ringmaster wears red evening tails, top hat, waxed moustache and uses a riding crop. He is immaculate—perhaps he doubles with Mr Fire Eater.

The High Court Judge is straight from *Trial by Jury* in appearance.

The Adult Villagers wear bright clothing with bright patches as though picturesque Neapolitan peasants.

The School Children are the same as Lampwick.

The Urchins are almost as the urchins in *Oliver Twist*, but once upon a time their rags have been bright-coloured Italian clothes.

The Funland People are in fact the Villagers and Juveniles wearing "Continental pierrot" costumes that are brightly coloured one piece costumes with pom-poms down the front and pierrot skullcaps, or clown hats shaped like a small dunce's cap. These costumes can be worn over the Villager costumes if need be. They wear domino masks of the same colour, as these Adult and Juvenile circus people at Funland must not seem to be honest Villagers.

When watching the offstage storn in Act II and singing the sea shanties, the Villagers just put on comedy sou'westers, macintoshes, battered hats, scarves and wellington boots over their basic Villager costumes.

Transformation to Donkeys. Pinocchio and Lampwick exit and then re-enter in the various phases of donkey costume (see script). The problem of the donkey forelegs is solved by their wearing grey or brown shirts that have extremely long sleeves hanging well below their hands. They hold a stick in each hand that is roughly two feet long and has the grey or brown material attached to it, so that each stick becomes a floppy tube. The lads have to bend forward and (the hands being hidden by material as explained) the "tube/forelegs" now look convincing. The lads' trousers (back legs), shirts (body) and forelegs are the same coloured material, the forelegs being first their sleeves and then the tube/sticks as explained.

Finally various Directors have asked about the famous "nose growing" scene. Don't think of this as belonging to the make-up department, but merely add three different sized prop noses over Pinocchio's own nose (he is dressed as a donkey in this part of the story, as you know). Let the elastic holding the prop nose to his head be the same colour as his donkey head-dress and the three different sized noses be the colour of his face—this scene is deliberately set behind the cage bars so that the elastic will not be noticed—and remember that the third nose should be really long, about three feet!

PRODUCTION NOTE

This will seem awkward at rehearsals, but make sure that Mr Fire Eater, the Coachman, the Ringmaster (who is sometimes also played by Mr Fire Eater), the Fairy, Mr Cricket and the Judge speak almost every single line directly to the audience and not to those on stage. These parts need playing stylistically in this type of musical—and the audience can hear their dialogue so much better this way. In particular Mr Fire Eater, the Ringmaster, and the Coachman should speak almost entirely to the audience—and with nasty relish of course!

COPYRIGHT INFORMATION

(See also page ii)

This play is fully protected under the Copyright Laws of the British Commonwealth of Nations, the United States of America and all countries of the Berne and Universal Copyright Conventions.

All rights including Stage, Motion Picture, Radio, Television, Public Reading, and Translation into Foreign Languages, are strictly reserved.

No part of this publication may lawfully be reproduced in ANY form or by any means — photocopying, typescript, recording (including video-recording), manuscript, electronic, mechanical, or otherwise—or be transmitted or stored in a retrieval system, without prior permission.

Licences for amateur performances are issued subject to the understanding that it shall be made clear in all advertising matter that the audience will witness an amateur performance; that the names of the authors of the plays shall be included on all programmes; and that the integrity of the authors' work will be preserved.

The Royalty Fee is subject to contract and subject to variation at the sole discretion of Samuel French Ltd.

In Theatres or Halls seating Four Hundred or more the fee will be subject to negotiation.

In Territories Overseas the fee quoted above may not apply. A fee will be quoted on application to our local authorized agent, or if there is no such agent, on application to Samuel French Ltd, London.

VIDEO-RECORDING OF AMATEUR PRODUCTIONS

Please note that the copyright laws governing video-recording are extremely complex and that it should not be assumed that any play may be video-recorded for whatever purpose without first obtaining the permission of the appropriate agents. The fact that a play is published by Samuel French Ltd does not indicate that video rights are available or that Samuel French Ltd controls such rights.

MADE AND PRINTED IN GREAT BRITAIN BY
LATIMER TREND & COMPANY LTD PLYMOUTH

MADE IN ENGLAND